EYEWITNESS VISUAL DICTIONARIES

THE VISUAL
DICTIONARY *of*
ANCIENT
CIVILIZATIONS

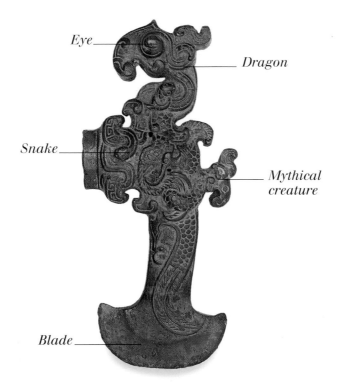

Eye

Dragon

Snake

Mythical creature

Blade

CHINESE RITUAL AX

Worker
mixing
grain

Worker
pulping grain

Beer jar

**EGYPTIAN MODEL OF WORKERS
MAKING BEER**

Eye
protector

Studded
decoration

**ROMAN HORSE
ARMOR**

Owl with
"ears"

Post with
flared top

Handle

Splayed leg

CHINESE RITUAL VESSEL

Goddess

Bird

MINOAN PENDANT

**MAYAN VESSEL DECORATION
SHOWING THE BALLGAME**

Moon

Red Sun

Gateway
to heaven

Owner of
the tomb

Dragon

Giant holding
up the
terrestrial
world

CHINESE SILK BANNER

Ballgame player

Glyph

Black body paint

Protection for one foot

Rubber ball

THE VISUAL
DICTIONARY *of*
ANCIENT
CIVILIZATIONS

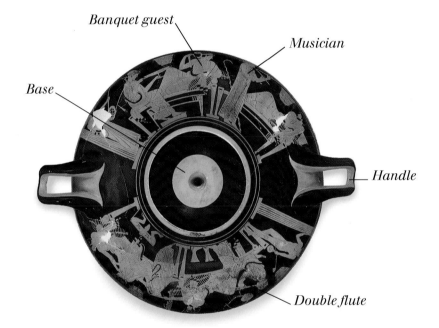

Banquet guest

Musician

Base

Handle

Double flute

**GREEK KYLIX
(DRINKING CUP)**

Bird headdress

*Ballgame
player*

Protection for one knee

A DK PUBLISHING BOOK

ART EDITOR CLARE SHEDDEN
DESIGNER SUSAN KNIGHT

PROJECT EDITOR LOUISE TUCKER
EDITOR EMILY HILL
CONSULTANT EDITORS JAMES HARPUR, CHRIS SCARRE,
ANTHONY SHELTON, GREGORY IRVINE, T. RICHARD BLURTON

U.S. EDITOR JILL HAMILTON
U.S. CONSULTANTS KIM BENZEL, JAYMIE L. BRAUER, JOHN R. FINLAY,
ROSS HASSIG, MIYAKO IOSHINAGA, MICHAEL MOSELEY, CATHERINE ROEHRIT,
CHARLES SPENCER, DAVID HURST THOMAS, NANCY THOMPSON

MANAGING ART EDITOR PHILIP GILDERDALE
MANAGING EDITOR RUTH MIDGLEY

ILLUSTRATIONS MALTINGS PARTNERSHIP

PRODUCTION HILARY STEPHENS

Lapith woman seeking refuge at a shrine

Statue of goddess

Lapith youth attacking centaur

Panther skin hanging on a tree, indicating a sacred grove

Lapith woman

Centaur

**FRIEZE SHOWING LAPITHS AND CENTAURS
FIGHTING, FROM THE TEMPLE AT BASSAE, GREECE**

FIRST AMERICAN EDITION, 1994

4 6 8 10 9 7 5 3

Published in the United States by
DK PUBLISHING, INC., 95 MADISON AVENUE
NEW YORK, NEW YORK 10016

VISIT US ON THE WORLD WIDE WEB AT
HTTP://WWW.DK.COM

LIBRARY OF CONGRESS CATALOGING-IN-PUBLICATION DATA

THE VISUAL DICTIONARY OF ANCIENT CIVILIZATIONS. — 1ST AMERICAN ED.
p. cm. — (EYEWITNESS VISUAL DICTIONARIES)
INCLUDES INDEX.

ISBN 1-56458-701-0
1. CIVILIZATION, ANCIENT—DICTIONARIES. 2. CIVILIZATION, ANCIENT—PICTORIAL WORKS.
I. SERIES.

CB311.V584 1994
930'.03—dc20

94-8395
CIP

REPRODUCED BY COLOURSCAN, SINGAPORE
PRINTED AND BOUND IN VERONA, ITALY, BY ARNOLDO MONDADORI

Contents

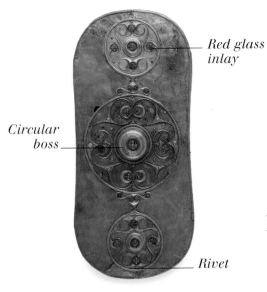

Red glass inlay

Circular boss

Rivet

CELTIC BRONZE SHIELD

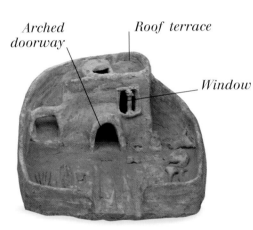

Arched doorway

Roof terrace

Window

EGYPTIAN MODEL OF A HOUSE

Topknot

Hair ornament

Silk robe

CHINESE TOMB FIGURES

Feline deity

Paw

Seated figure

ANDEAN POT

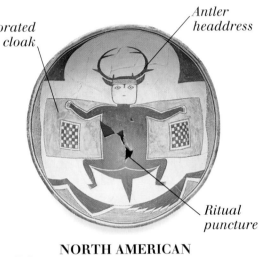

Decorated cloak

Antler headdress

Ritual puncture

NORTH AMERICAN BOWL

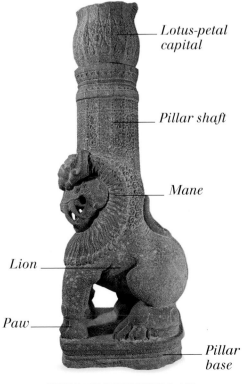

Lotus-petal capital

Pillar shaft

Mane

Lion

Paw

Pillar base

INDIAN LION PILLAR

Mesopotamia: everyday life

Milk

Shaven head

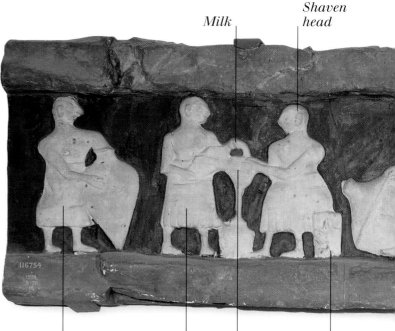

MESOPOTAMIA, IN THE MIDDLE EAST, was the site of one of the earliest known civilizations. Between 4000 and 3000 B.C., the Sumerians of southern Mesopotamia built the first cities in the world on the fertile plain between the Tigris and Euphrates rivers. Sumerian cities, such as Uruk and Ur, were enclosed by walls and had temples raised on top of ziggurats—huge, stepped pyramids with flat tops. The Sumerians were efficient farmers, using irrigation to water pastures and crops. Domesticated animals, such as goats and cows, were reared on the pastures and provided a constant supply of meat, milk, butter, and skins. The Sumerians also developed one of the earliest known forms of writing, which they used to keep records of livestock, food, and other goods. Scribes (professional writers) used a sharpened reed stylus to inscribe simple pictures, known as pictographs, on clay tablets. Gradually the pictographs became more abstract, eventually developing into a new form of script, known as cuneiform, which was written using styluses with wedge-shaped tips. Documents and letters written in cuneiform were "signed" with a cylinder seal—a small, engraved, cylinder-shaped stone—that was rolled across clay tablets to produce a continuous pattern.

CYLINDER SEAL

Worker stirring milk

Fleece garment

Strainer

Stool

CLAY TABLET WITH PICTOGRAPHIC RECORD OF DAILY RATIONS

Symbol for a commodity

Symbol for a commodity

Symbol for one unit

Symbol for day one

Symbol for day two

Symbol for day three

Part of symbol for day four

Symbol for day five

Symbol for a commodity

Symbol for 10 units

Symbol for a commodity

Symbol for a commodity

CLAY TABLETS WITH EARLY PICTOGRAPHS

Symbol for 10

Symbol for 10

Animal, possibly a sheep

Animal, possibly a goat

CAST OF FRIEZE FROM TEMPLE OF NINHURSAG, TELL 'UBAID

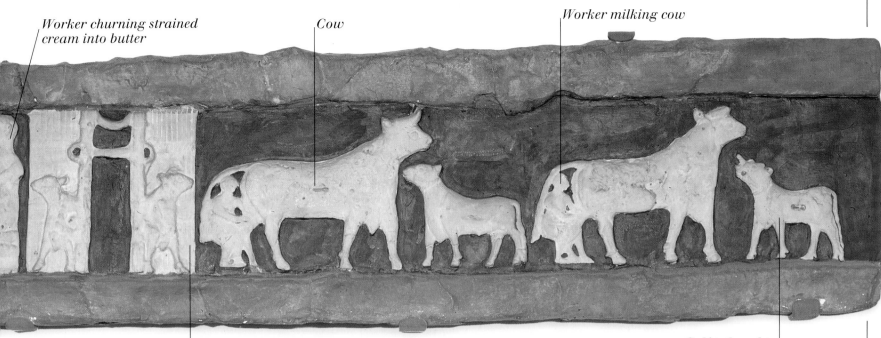

Worker churning strained cream into butter

Cow

Worker milking cow

Cowshed

Calf tethered to prevent suckling

COPPER FIGURINE WITH CUNEIFORM TEXT FROM TEMPLE OF INANNA, URUK

Builder's basket

Peg-shaped base

Cuneiform dedication stating that King Ur-Nammu built a temple for the goddess Inanna "and restored it as it should be"

CYLINDER SEALS WITH IMPRESSIONS

GYPSUM SEAL

Recipient of offering

Offering of an ear of corn

Offering of implement

Recipient of offering

Person drinking beer

Goat

Lion

ARAGONITE SEAL

Goat being attacked

Bull being attacked

Lion

Bull-man stabbing lion

Scorpion

GREENSTONE SEAL

Goddess

Hash-hamer, owner of the seal

Moon, symbol of god Nanna

King

Cuneiform inscription "Ur-Nammu, strong man, King of Ur: Hash-hamer, governor of the city of Ishkum-Sin, is your servant"

7

Mesopotamia: the graves at Ur

THE SUMERIAN CITY OF UR was one of the world's first cities. Within its walls were important graves, dating from around 2500 B.C. Some contained spectacular treasures that reveal the skill and artistry of the Sumerians. There were functional items, such as chariots and rein rings, and decorative objects, such as two stands in the form of a goat behind a flowering shrub. The most elaborate graves were stone or mud brick chambers, some of which contained not only the body of the tomb owner, but also those of many attendants who were either sacrificed or committed ritual suicide. Many attendants went into the grave wearing fine jewelry and playing musical instruments. One of the most interesting objects, the so-called "Standard of Ur," is a decorated wooden box, which may have been part of a lyre. Its two largest sides are known as the War side, because it shows soldiers and war chariots, and the Peace side, which probably shows a celebratory banquet.

HEADDRESS AND JEWELRY

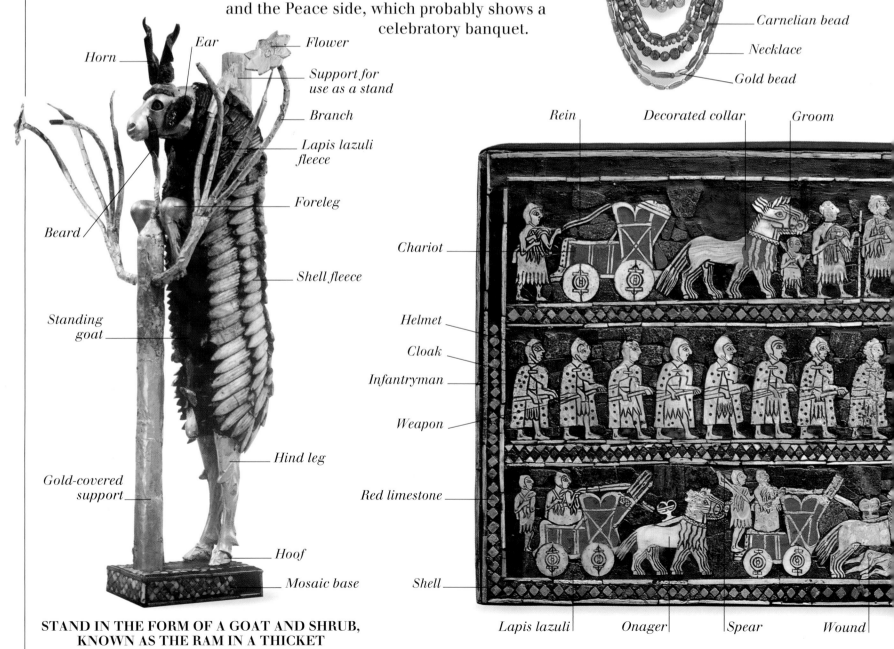

Gold rosette

Three-pronged headdress

Gold leaf

Crescent-shaped earring

Lapis lazuli and gold collar

Lapis lazuli bead

Carnelian bead

Necklace

Gold bead

Horn

Ear

Flower

Support for use as a stand

Branch

Lapis lazuli fleece

Foreleg

Beard

Shell fleece

Standing goat

Gold-covered support

Hind leg

Hoof

Mosaic base

STAND IN THE FORM OF A GOAT AND SHRUB, KNOWN AS THE RAM IN A THICKET

Rein

Decorated collar

Groom

Chariot

Helmet

Cloak

Infantryman

Weapon

Red limestone

Shell

Lapis lazuli

Onager

Spear

Wound

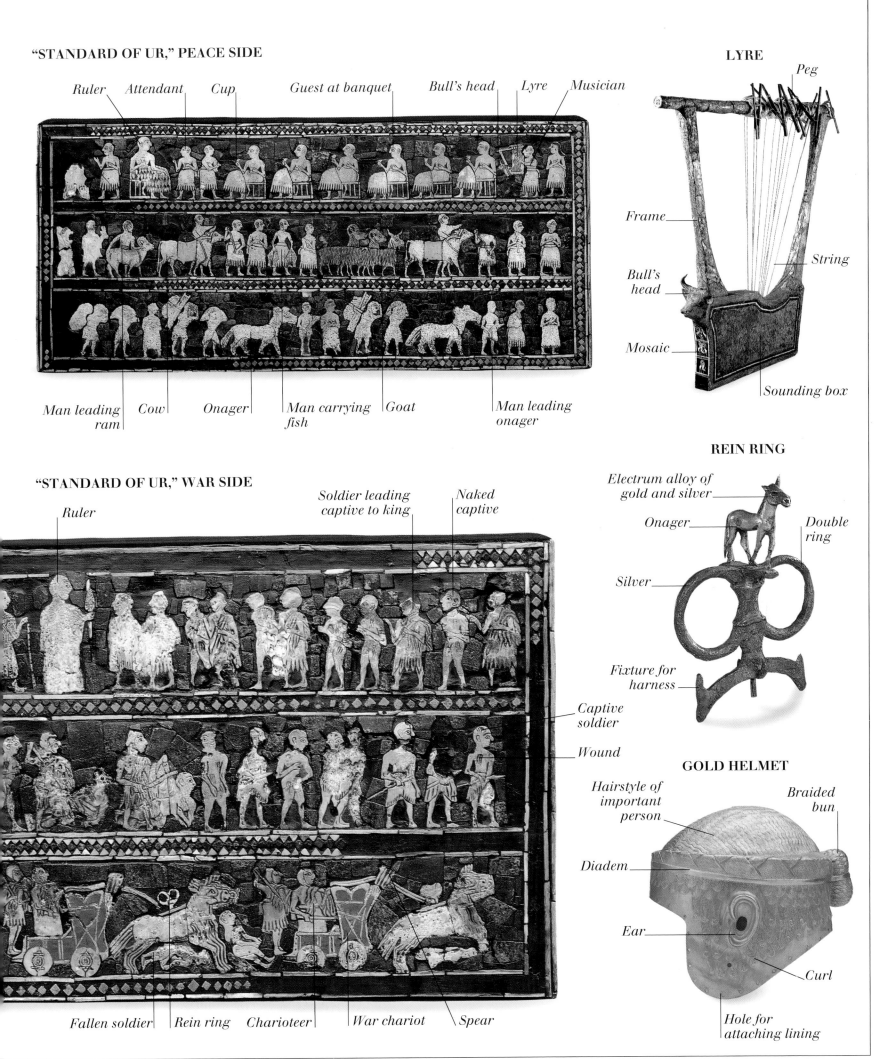

"STANDARD OF UR," PEACE SIDE

Ruler Attendant Cup Guest at banquet Bull's head Lyre Musician

Man leading ram Cow Onager Man carrying fish Goat Man leading onager

"STANDARD OF UR," WAR SIDE

Ruler Soldier leading captive to king Naked captive Captive soldier Wound

Fallen soldier Rein ring Charioteer War chariot Spear

LYRE

Peg Frame String Bull's head Mosaic Sounding box

REIN RING

Electrum alloy of gold and silver Onager Double ring Silver Fixture for harness

GOLD HELMET

Hairstyle of important person Braided bun Diadem Ear Curl Hole for attaching lining

Egypt: pyramids and temples

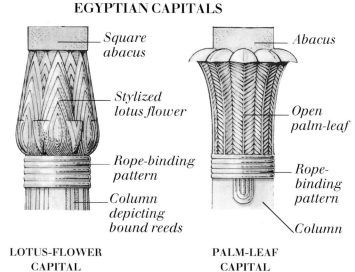

Square abacus

Stylized lotus flower

Rope-binding pattern

Column depicting bound reeds

LOTUS-FLOWER CAPITAL

Abacus

Open palm-leaf

Rope-binding pattern

Column

PALM-LEAF CAPITAL

THE FOUNDATIONS of Egyptian civilization were laid in about 3000 B.C. when Egypt was first unified under the control of a single king. The king, known as the pharaoh, controlled the vast resources of the Egyptian state and used these for ambitious building projects. The earlier Egyptian rulers built enormous pyramid tombs for themselves. Later kings concentrated their efforts on temples, the largest of which had hypostyle halls with painted columns and capitals in the form of a lotus flower, papyrus plant, or palm leaf. The first Egyptian pyramid was built at Saqqara as a stepped structure. The Meidum pyramid was originally built in seven steps around a central core, and the whole building was faced with limestone to form smooth sides. This pyramid was unstable, however, and the outer layers soon fell away. The Bent pyramid at Dahshur was built with a greater inward slope on its upper part for stability. The most impressive pyramids are those at Giza, which are smooth-sided or "true" pyramids.

SPHINX AND KING KHAFRE'S PYRAMID

THE HYPOSTYLE HALL, TEMPLE OF AMON-RE, KARNAK

Architrave

Stone slab forming flat roof of side aisle

Cornice decorated with cavetto molding

Socle

Papyrus motif

Amon-Re, principal god

Hathor, a goddess

Cartouche (oval frame) containing the titles of King Ramesses II

Aisle running north-south

Central nave

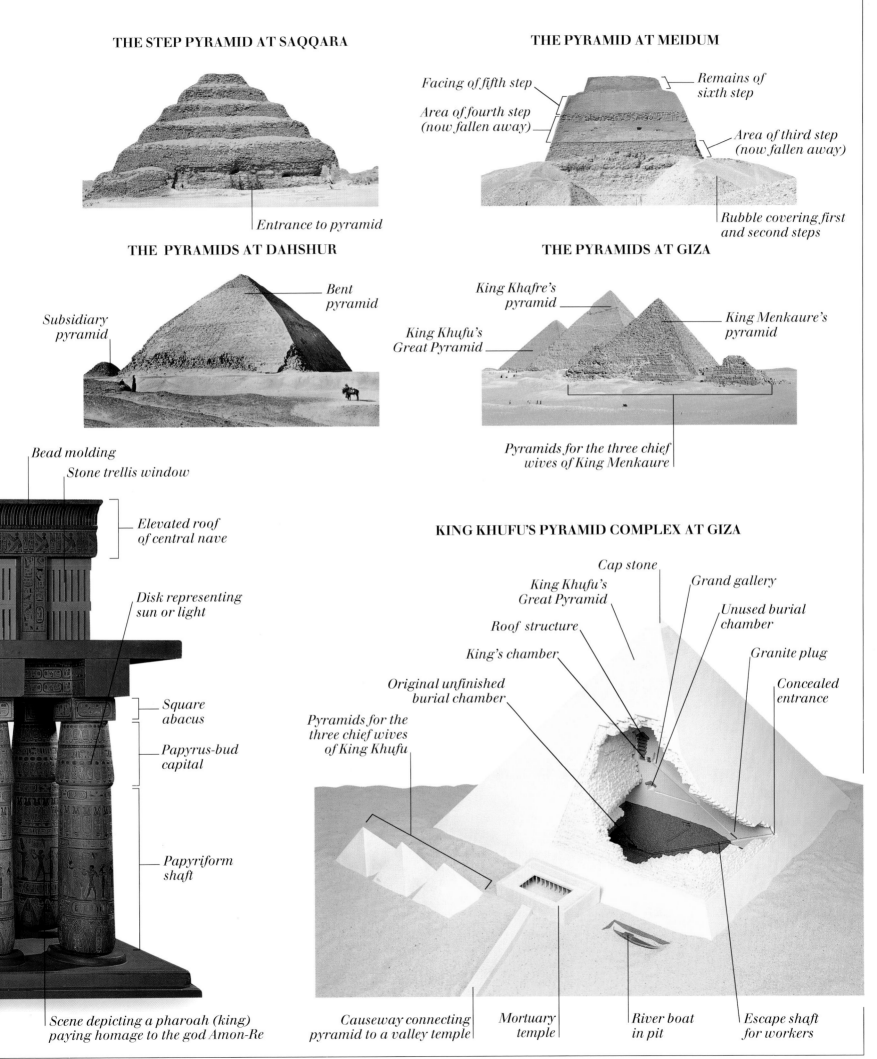

THE STEP PYRAMID AT SAQQARA

Entrance to pyramid

THE PYRAMID AT MEIDUM

Facing of fifth step

Remains of sixth step

Area of fourth step (now fallen away)

Area of third step (now fallen away)

Rubble covering first and second steps

THE PYRAMIDS AT DAHSHUR

Bent pyramid

Subsidiary pyramid

THE PYRAMIDS AT GIZA

King Khafre's pyramid

King Menkaure's pyramid

King Khufu's Great Pyramid

Pyramids for the three chief wives of King Menkaure

Bead molding

Stone trellis window

Elevated roof of central nave

Disk representing sun or light

Square abacus

Papyrus-bud capital

Papyriform shaft

Scene depicting a pharoah (king) paying homage to the god Amon-Re

KING KHUFU'S PYRAMID COMPLEX AT GIZA

Cap stone

King Khufu's Great Pyramid

Grand gallery

Unused burial chamber

Roof structure

Granite plug

King's chamber

Concealed entrance

Original unfinished burial chamber

Pyramids for the three chief wives of King Khufu

Causeway connecting pyramid to a valley temple

Mortuary temple

River boat in pit

Escape shaft for workers

Egypt: everyday life

FAIENCE DRINKING CUP

ANCIENT EGYPT was a bureaucratic and centralized state ruled by the pharaoh. He exacted taxes from his citizens to support the court as well as the religious and administrative systems. Careful records of produce and taxes were kept by professional writers known as scribes. All scribes and officials enjoyed a high status in Egyptian society. Other people with special skills, such as carpenters, jewelers, and sculptors, were valued as craftspeople, and some were employed to work directly for the state as royal artisans. Most of the population, however, were agricultural laborers or servants in the houses of the wealthy. Agricultural work included raising cattle on pasture lands and cultivating crops, such as barley and wheat, in the rich silt deposited by the annual flooding of the Nile River. As the floodwaters receded, laborers would have repaired the damage caused to bridges, roads, canals, and cultivation plots.

INLAID GOLD BRACELET

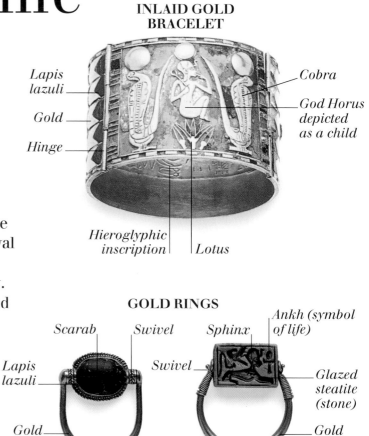

Lapis lazuli

Gold

Hinge

Cobra

God Horus depicted as a child

Hieroglyphic inscription

Lotus

GOLD RINGS

Scarab

Swivel

Sphinx

Ankh (symbol of life)

Lapis lazuli

Swivel

Glazed steatite (stone)

Gold

Gold

TOMB PAINTING SHOWING CRAFTSMEN AT WORK

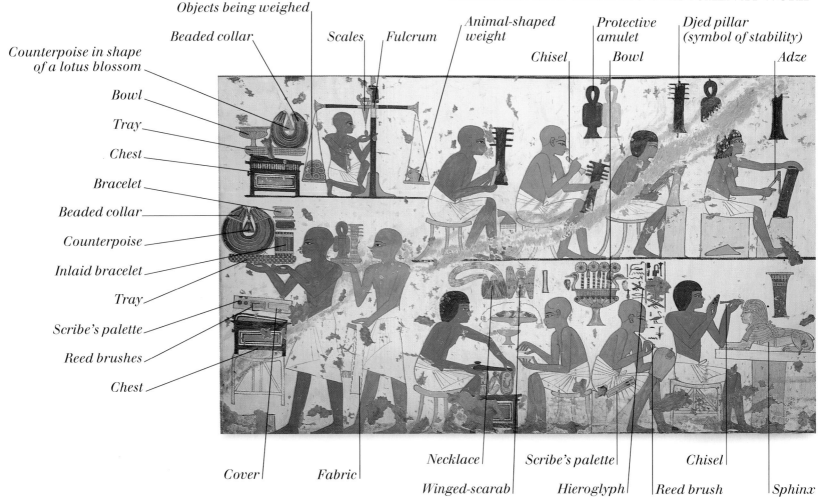

Objects being weighed

Beaded collar

Scales

Fulcrum

Animal-shaped weight

Protective amulet

Djed pillar (symbol of stability)

Counterpoise in shape of a lotus blossom

Chisel

Bowl

Adze

Bowl

Tray

Chest

Bracelet

Beaded collar

Counterpoise

Inlaid bracelet

Tray

Scribe's palette

Reed brushes

Chest

Cover

Fabric

Necklace

Winged-scarab

Scribe's palette

Hieroglyph

Chisel

Reed brush

Sphinx

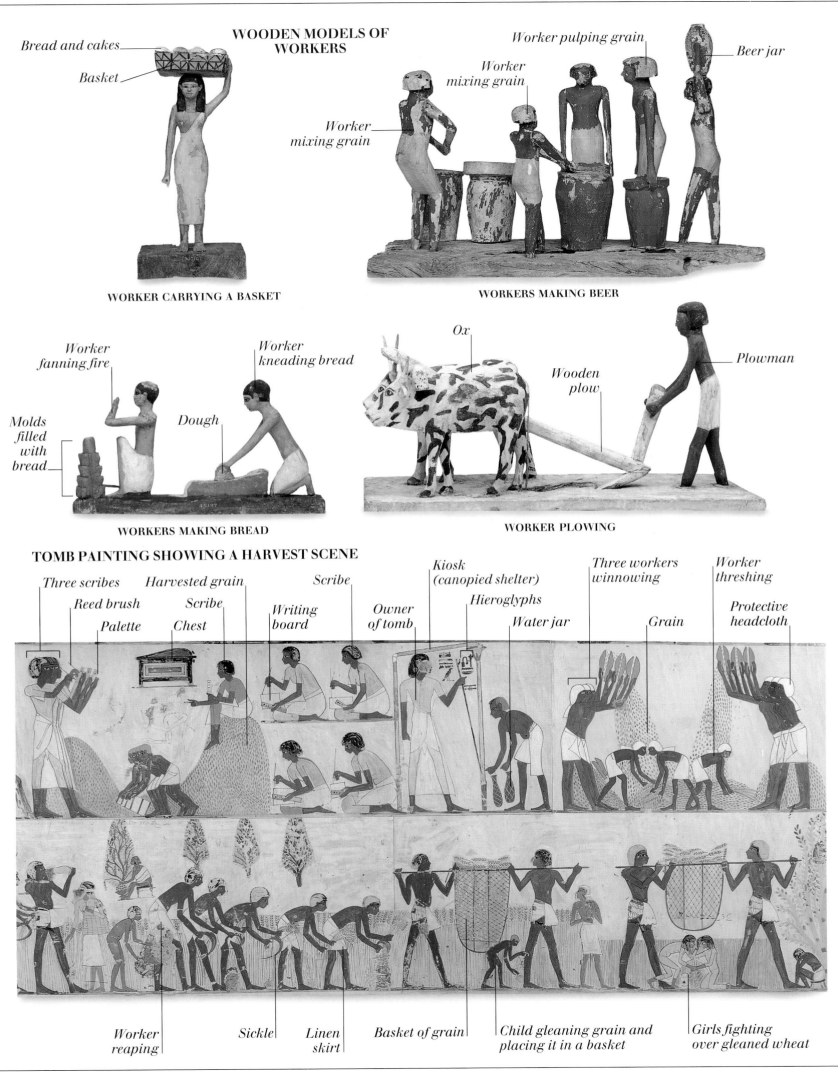

WOODEN MODELS OF WORKERS

Bread and cakes

Basket

Worker pulping grain

Beer jar

Worker mixing grain

Worker mixing grain

WORKER CARRYING A BASKET

WORKERS MAKING BEER

Worker fanning fire

Worker kneading bread

Molds filled with bread

Dough

Ox

Wooden plow

Plowman

WORKERS MAKING BREAD

WORKER PLOWING

TOMB PAINTING SHOWING A HARVEST SCENE

Three scribes

Reed brush

Palette

Harvested grain

Scribe

Chest

Writing board

Scribe

Owner of tomb

Kiosk (canopied shelter)

Hieroglyphs

Water jar

Three workers winnowing

Grain

Worker threshing

Protective headcloth

Worker reaping

Sickle

Linen skirt

Basket of grain

Child gleaning grain and placing it in a basket

Girls fighting over gleaned wheat

Egypt: death and the afterlife

EYE OF HORUS (WEDJAT EYE)

THE ANCIENT EGYPTIANS BELIEVED that when they died they journeyed to the world of the dead and enjoyed an afterlife. Every person had a spirit that survived death if the body was embalmed to preserve it. During embalming, the internal organs were removed and usually placed in four canopic jars, each of which was guarded by a son of the god Horus (Horus guided the deceased through the world of the dead). Even when the jars were not used to hold organs, dummy jars were put in the tombs as charms. The body was treated with preservatives and wrapped in linen bandages, among which were placed protective charms or amulets, such as the eye of Horus (also called the wedjat eye). The bandaged body—known as a mummy—was then fitted with a face mask and placed inside a mummy case, which was painted with religious images and texts, such as scenes from the Book of the Dead (a collection of texts and spells to help the deceased in the afterlife). Mummies were often buried with provisions for the world of the dead; these ranged from food and furniture to shabti figures—models of laborers who would work in the next world on behalf of the deceased.

SHABTI BOX

Imsety, human-headed son of Horus

Shabti figure

Lid

Painted wooden box

Lid

Shabti figure

Duamutef, jackal-headed son of Horus

Offerings to gods

Priestess Henutmehit, owner of shabti box

MUMMY CASE

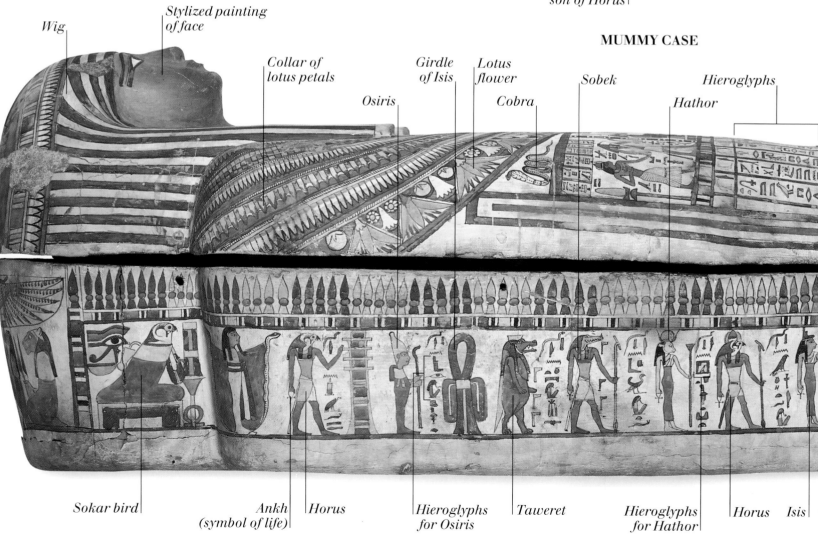

Wig

Stylized painting of face

Collar of lotus petals

Osiris

Girdle of Isis

Lotus flower

Cobra

Sobek

Hathor

Hieroglyphs

Sokar bird

Ankh (symbol of life)

Horus

Hieroglyphs for Osiris

Taweret

Hieroglyphs for Hathor

Horus

Isis

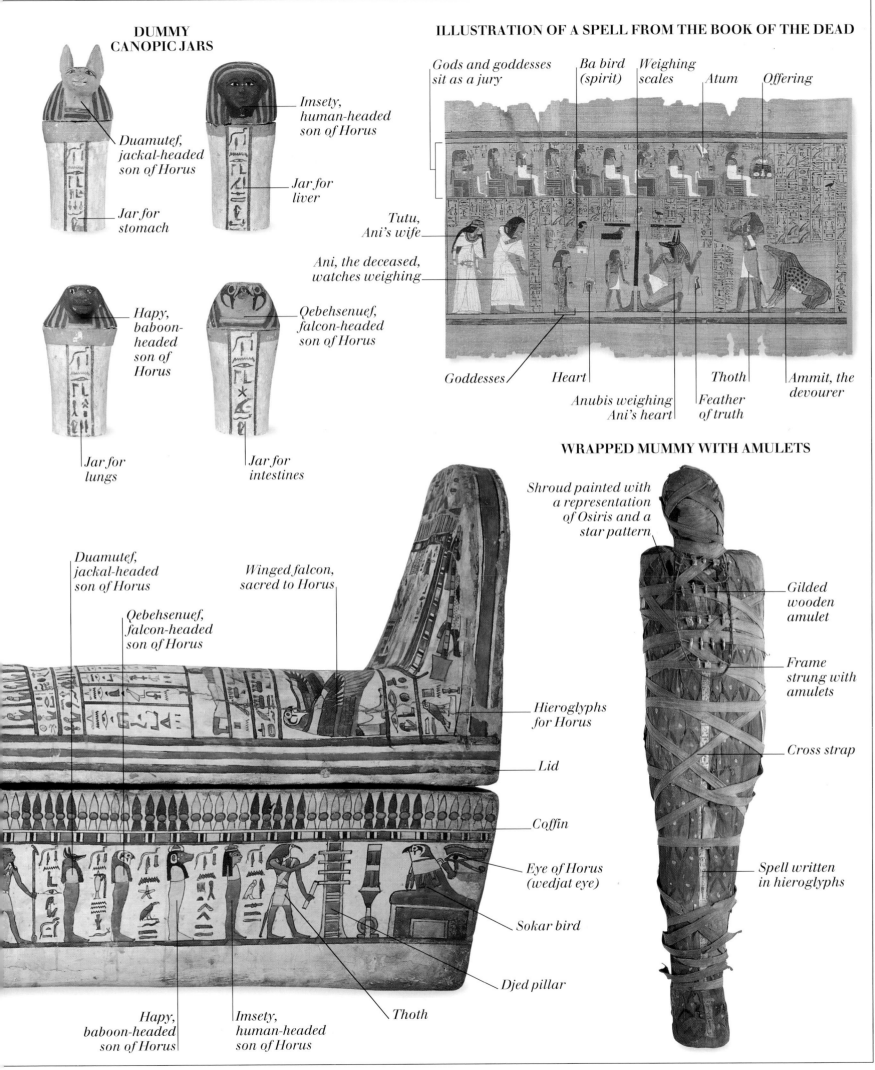

DUMMY CANOPIC JARS

Duamutef, jackal-headed son of Horus

Jar for stomach

Imsety, human-headed son of Horus

Jar for liver

Hapy, baboon-headed son of Horus

Qebehsenuef, falcon-headed son of Horus

Jar for lungs

Jar for intestines

ILLUSTRATION OF A SPELL FROM THE BOOK OF THE DEAD

Gods and goddesses sit as a jury

Ba bird (spirit)

Weighing scales

Atum

Offering

Tutu, Ani's wife

Ani, the deceased, watches weighing

Goddesses

Heart

Anubis weighing Ani's heart

Feather of truth

Thoth

Ammit, the devourer

WRAPPED MUMMY WITH AMULETS

Shroud painted with a representation of Osiris and a star pattern

Gilded wooden amulet

Frame strung with amulets

Cross strap

Spell written in hieroglyphs

Duamutef, jackal-headed son of Horus

Qebehsenuef, falcon-headed son of Horus

Winged falcon, sacred to Horus

Hieroglyphs for Horus

Lid

Coffin

Eye of Horus (wedjat eye)

Sokar bird

Djed pillar

Thoth

Hapy, baboon-headed son of Horus

Imsety, human-headed son of Horus

The Assyrians

THE WARLIKE ASSYRIANS were the dominant power in the Middle East from the ninth to the seventh century B.C., when they were defeated by the Medes (from the northwest of Iran) and the Babylonians (see pp. 18–19). From their heartland in northern Iraq around the Tigris River, the Assyrians carved out an empire that stretched from Egypt in the west to Iran in the east. Assyrian kings built magnificent palaces that had walls lined with carved stone slabs showing hunting, battle, and court scenes. In some of these carvings, the king was shown killing lions in a specially organized hunt. This action, depicted on the royal seal, symbolized his role as protector of the Assyrian people. The king was also the chief priest and played an important part in religious rituals. Statues of gods, known as household gods, were placed beneath the floors of palaces and houses to guard against evil spirits.

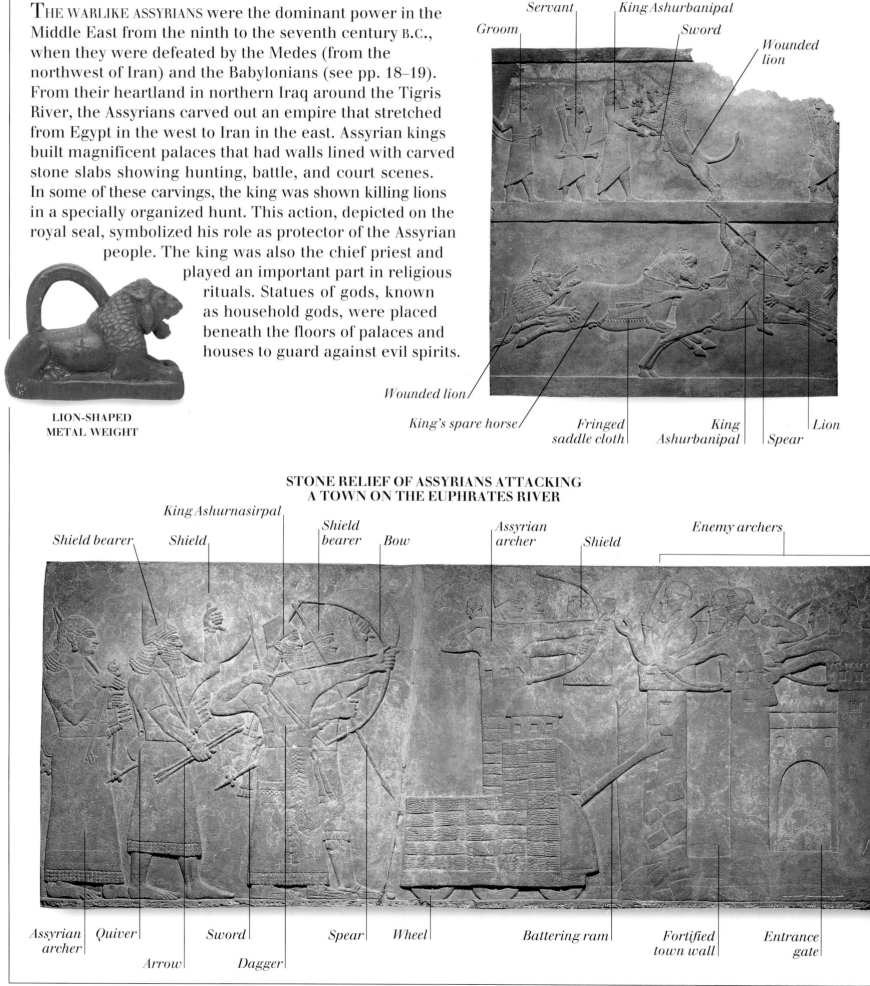

LION-SHAPED METAL WEIGHT

STONE RELIEF OF KING ASHURBANIPAL (668–627 B.C.) KILLING A LION

Servant

King Ashurbanipal

Groom

Sword

Wounded lion

Wounded lion

King's spare horse

Fringed saddle cloth

King Ashurbanipal

Spear

Lion

STONE RELIEF OF ASSYRIANS ATTACKING A TOWN ON THE EUPHRATES RIVER

King Ashurnasirpal

Shield bearer

Shield

Shield bearer

Bow

Assyrian archer

Shield

Enemy archers

Assyrian archer

Quiver

Sword

Spear

Wheel

Battering ram

Fortified town wall

Entrance gate

Arrow

Dagger

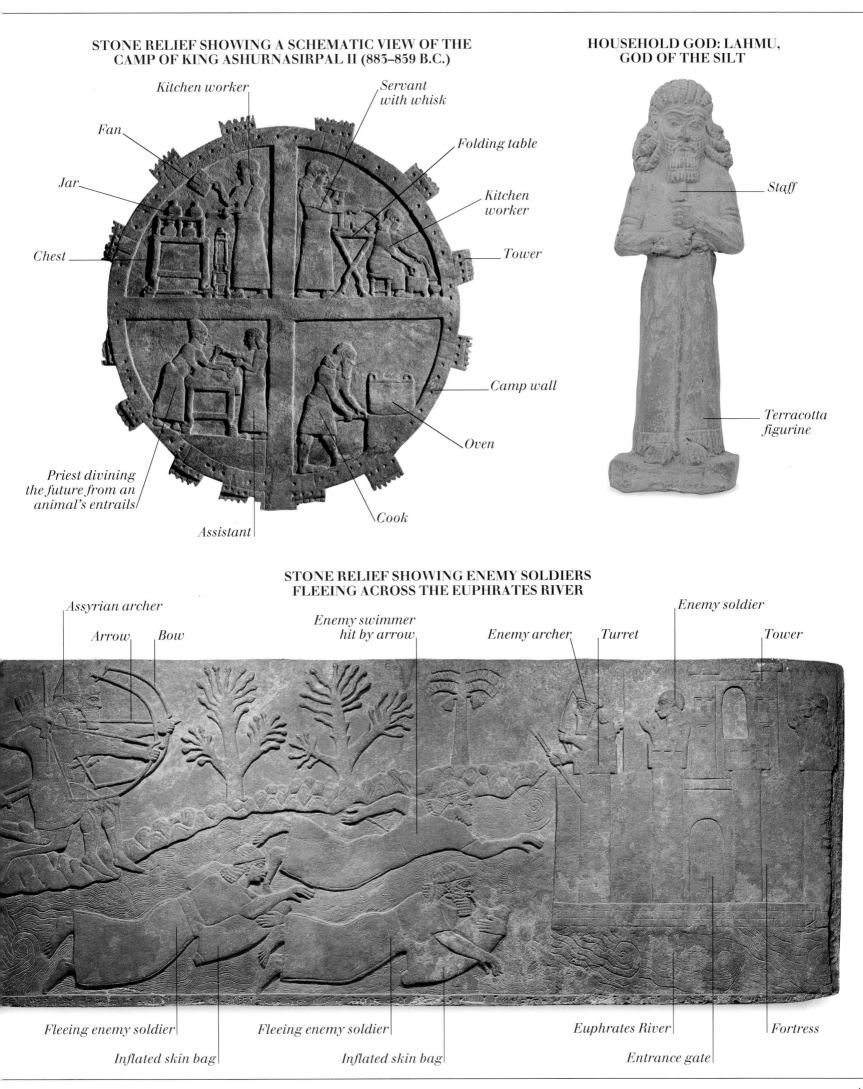

**STONE RELIEF SHOWING A SCHEMATIC VIEW OF THE
CAMP OF KING ASHURNASIRPAL II (883–859 B.C.)**

Kitchen worker

Servant
with whisk

Fan

Folding table

Jar

Kitchen
worker

Chest

Tower

Camp wall

Oven

Priest divining
the future from an
animal's entrails

Cook

Assistant

**HOUSEHOLD GOD: LAHMU,
GOD OF THE SILT**

Staff

Terracotta
figurine

**STONE RELIEF SHOWING ENEMY SOLDIERS
FLEEING ACROSS THE EUPHRATES RIVER**

Assyrian archer

Enemy soldier

Arrow

Bow

Enemy swimmer
hit by arrow

Enemy archer

Turret

Tower

Fleeing enemy soldier

Fleeing enemy soldier

Euphrates River

Fortress

Inflated skin bag

Inflated skin bag

Entrance gate

17

The Babylonians

SITUATED ON THE EUPHRATES RIVER, in central Mesopotamia, Babylon became the capital of a great Near Eastern empire at the end of the seventh century B.C. This empire survived until its defeat by the Persians in 539 B.C. During this period the city of Babylon was rebuilt by two kings, Nabopolassar (625–605 B.C.) and Nebuchadnezzar II (604–562 B.C.). The Hanging Gardens of Babylon were created over terraces and were renowned as one of the seven wonders of the ancient world. Babylon's splendid new walls, temples, palaces, and gateways were each named after a deity. The beautifully tiled Ishtar Gate, for example, bears the name of the goddess of love and war. The most important Babylonian deity was Marduk, but there were many others, including the Moon god Sin and the Sun god Shamash. Symbols of the deities were carved on boundary stones, which marked property divisions and recorded legal contracts concerning land allocation and tax concessions. The Babylonians were expert mathematicians and astrologers, and mapped out their view of the world with Babylon at the center.

PLAQUE SHOWING A MAGICAL SPIRIT

SECTION OF THE BRICK FRIEZE FROM THE PROCESSIONAL WAY

Color-glazed brick relief

Lion, symbol of the goddess Ishtar

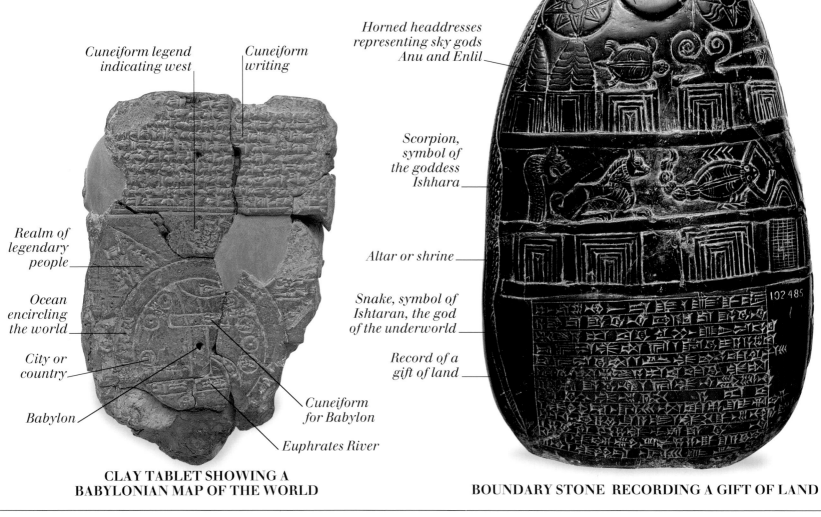

Cuneiform legend indicating west

Cuneiform writing

Realm of legendary people

Ocean encircling the world

City or country

Babylon

Cuneiform for Babylon

Euphrates River

CLAY TABLET SHOWING A BABYLONIAN MAP OF THE WORLD

Sun, symbol of the Sun god Shamash

Moon, symbol of the Moon god Sin

Stylus representing Nabu, god of writing

Star, symbol of Ishtar, goddess of love and war

Horned headdresses representing sky gods Anu and Enlil

Scorpion, symbol of the goddess Ishhara

Altar or shrine

Snake, symbol of Ishtaran, the god of the underworld

Record of a gift of land

BOUNDARY STONE RECORDING A GIFT OF LAND

THE ISHTAR GATE

Color-glazed
brick frieze

Stepped
battlement

Ishtar Gate

Fortified tower

Stepped
battlement

Fortified
wall

Color-glazed
brick frieze of lions

Processional Way

**THE ISHTAR GATE AND THE
PROCESSIONAL WAY**

Color-glazed brick
frieze of rosettes

Fortified tower

Gateway

Color-glazed brick
frieze of rosettes

Dragon, symbol of
the god Marduk

Bull, symbol of
the god Adad

The Persians

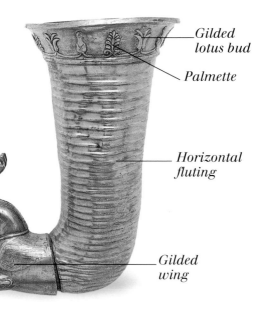

Gilded
lotus bud

Palmette

Horizontal
fluting

Horn

Griffin

Gilded
wing

FOUNDED BY CYRUS THE GREAT in 550 B.C., the Persian Empire under the Achaemenid dynasty was the largest yet seen in the ancient world. From their heartland in southwestern Iran, Persian rulers governed territories that eventually stretched from Libya in the west to the borders of India in the east. The empire reached its peak under King Darius I, a ruler renowned for his fairness, who reigned from 522 to 486 B.C. Darius, an excellent organizer, divided the empire into a number of provinces called satrapies, each with its own governor. The administration of the empire was made easier by a network of roads, including the Royal Road that stretched from Susa in Iran to Sardis in Turkey. The Persian king commanded a large, well-organized army, and had an elite bodyguard, known as the Ten Thousand Immortals. The Persian nobility were renowned for their love of luxury, since they enjoyed hunting, eating and drinking, and wearing fine clothes and jewelry. A hoard of treasure, discovered by the Oxus River in central Asia, illustrates the skill of craftsmen serving the Achaemenid rulers. One of the most spectacular objects was a gold armlet with ends in the form of griffins, mythological creatures with the wings and beak of an eagle and the body of a lion.

STONE RELIEF OF
A PERSIAN HEAD

**GOLD ARMLET FROM THE
OXUS TREASURE**

Horn

Beak

Ear

Griffin

Wing

Setting
for inlay
(now lost)

Paw

**GILDED SILVER DISC SHOWING A HUNTING
SCENE FROM THE OXUS TREASURE**

Wounded
wild goat

Fringed
saddlecloth

Deer

Broken
spear

Hare

Hunter

Horse

Boss pierced with holes

**GOLD MODEL CHARIOT FROM
THE OXUS TREASURE**

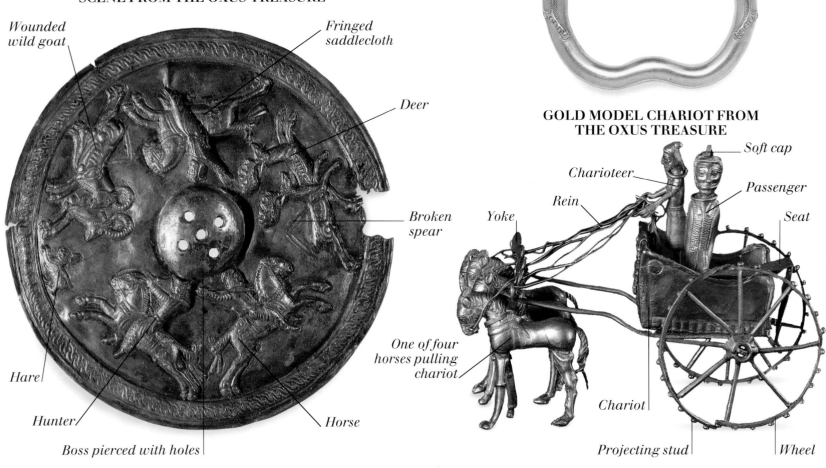

Soft cap

Charioteer

Passenger

Rein

Yoke

Seat

One of four
horses pulling
chariot

Chariot

Projecting stud

Wheel

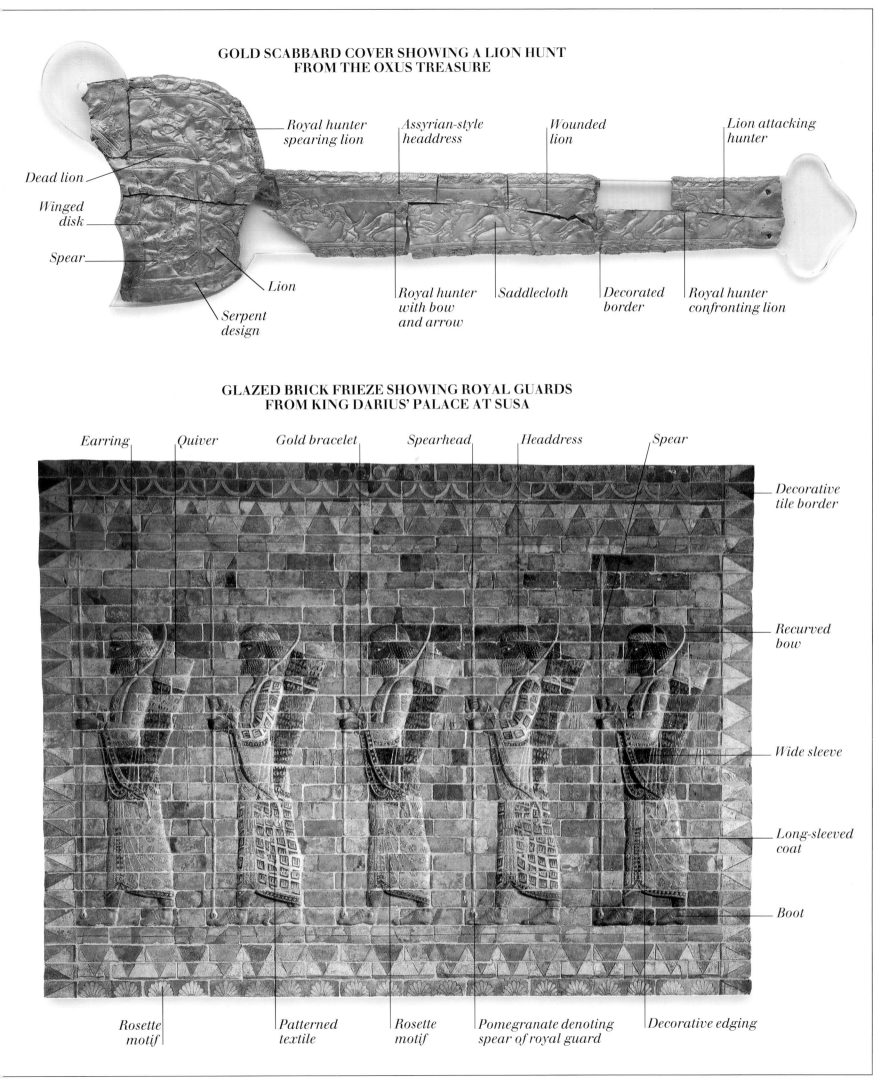

**GOLD SCABBARD COVER SHOWING A LION HUNT
FROM THE OXUS TREASURE**

Royal hunter spearing lion

Assyrian-style headdress

Wounded lion

Lion attacking hunter

Dead lion

Winged disk

Spear

Lion

Serpent design

Royal hunter with bow and arrow

Saddlecloth

Decorated border

Royal hunter confronting lion

**GLAZED BRICK FRIEZE SHOWING ROYAL GUARDS
FROM KING DARIUS' PALACE AT SUSA**

Earring

Quiver

Gold bracelet

Spearhead

Headdress

Spear

Decorative tile border

Recurved bow

Wide sleeve

Long-sleeved coat

Boot

Rosette motif

Patterned textile

Rosette motif

Pomegranate denoting spear of royal guard

Decorative edging

The Celts

CERAMIC DISH,
GERMANY

FROM THE EIGHTH CENTURY B.C. to the first
century A.D., Celtic people dominated much
of Europe from the Atlantic Ocean to the
Carpathian Mountains, and from Britain to
northern Italy. The Celts were divided into
a number of different tribes, who spoke similar
languages and had social, religious, and cultural
practices in common. The Greeks and Romans gave
the Celts their collective name and traded with them.
Wine and luxury goods, such as bronze vessels, were imported from
Greece and Rome, in return for cattle, skins, slaves, and salt.
Celtic culture is divided into two main phases known as Hallstatt
(c.800–500 B.C.) and La Tène (c.500 B.C.–A.D. 50). Chieftains of the
Hallstatt and early La Tène period lived in fortified hilltop settlements,
and buried their dead under mounds with bronze vessels, furniture,
and other provisions. Hallstatt artisans drew realistic animals on
pottery, bronze vessels, and wagon shafts. La Tène culture is noted
for its mainly abstract art forms. Shields, mirrors, the handles of
daggers and sheaths, and other objects were decorated with swirling
patterns typically made from circular lines and floral motifs.

Spring

Curved
decorative
foot

Pin

**BRONZE FIBULA (PIN),
SWITZERLAND**

Attachment for pin
(now broken)

Creature

**SILVER FIBULA
(PIN), IBERIA**

Recumbent dog

Duck

Stopper inlaid
with red glass

Dog's head

La Tène-
style pattern

Spout

Neck

Etruscan
flagon shape

Dog-shaped
handle

Decorative
coral inlay

**BRONZE FLAGON,
BASSE-YUTZ, FRANCE**

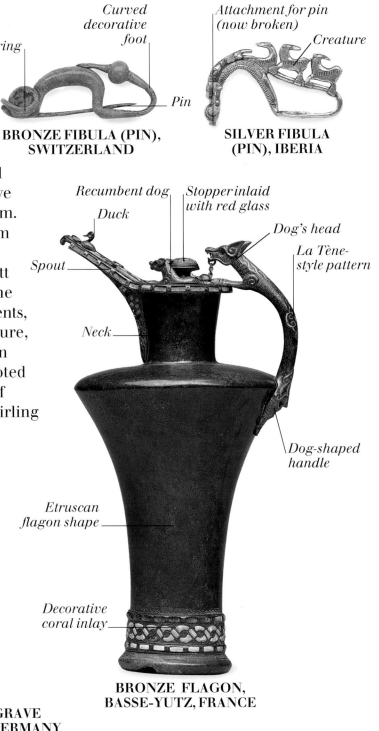

RECONSTRUCTED WAGON FROM THE GRAVE OF A CHIEFTAIN, HOCHDORF, GERMANY

Spoke

Wood covered with
iron and bronze plates

Pole for attaching
to draft animal

Wheel

Hub

BRONZE COUCH FROM THE GRAVE OF A CHIEFTAIN, HOCHDORF, GERMANY

Wagon

Horse

Punched-dot
decoration

Fighter
or dancer

Human figure

Spear

Shield

Rivet

Couch
support

Female
figurine

Wheel

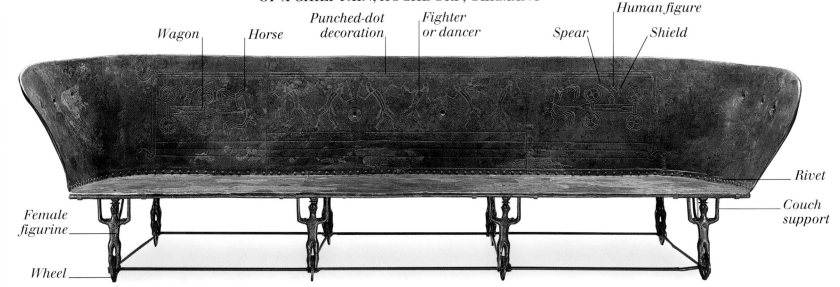

22

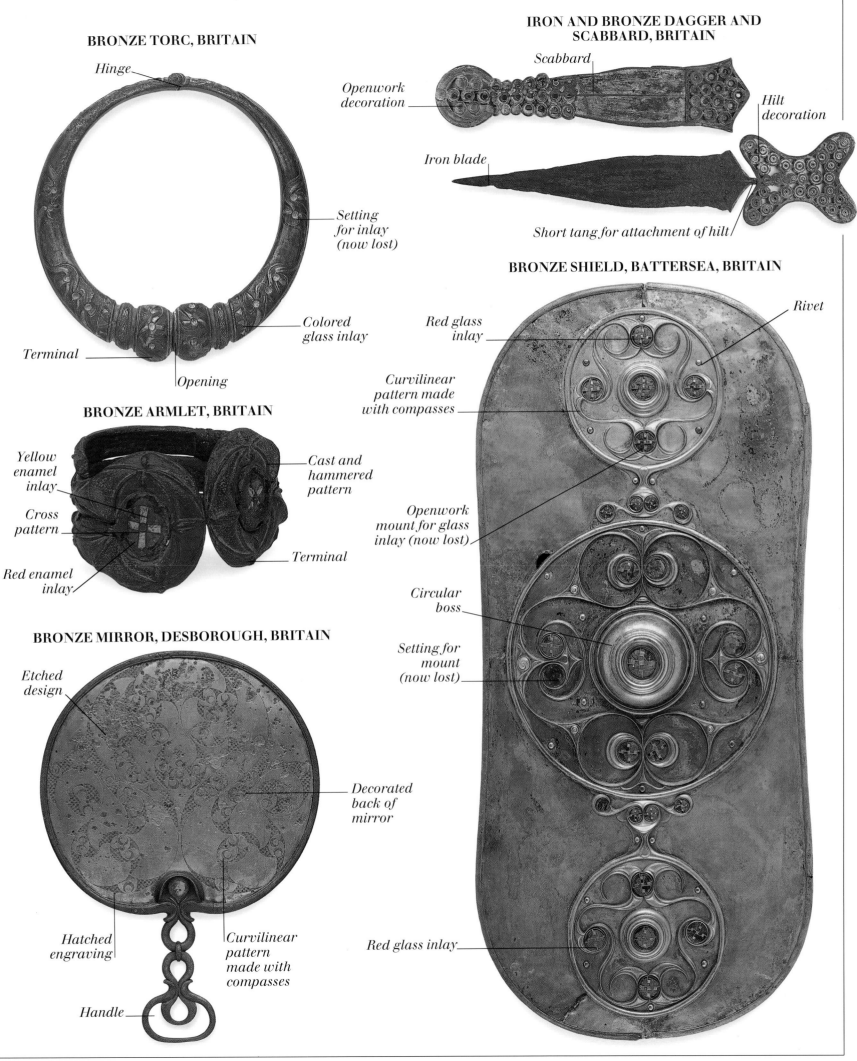

BRONZE TORC, BRITAIN

Hinge

Setting
for inlay
(now lost)

Terminal

Colored
glass inlay

Opening

BRONZE ARMLET, BRITAIN

Yellow
enamel
inlay

Cast and
hammered
pattern

Cross
pattern

Red enamel
inlay

Terminal

BRONZE MIRROR, DESBOROUGH, BRITAIN

Etched
design

Decorated
back of
mirror

Hatched
engraving

Curvilinear
pattern
made with
compasses

Handle

**IRON AND BRONZE DAGGER AND
SCABBARD, BRITAIN**

Scabbard

Openwork
decoration

Hilt
decoration

Iron blade

Short tang for attachment of hilt

BRONZE SHIELD, BATTERSEA, BRITAIN

Red glass
inlay

Rivet

Curvilinear
pattern made
with compasses

Openwork
mount for glass
inlay (now lost)

Circular
boss

Setting for
mount
(now lost)

Red glass inlay

Minoans and Mycenaeans

PALACE OF
KNOSSOS, CRETE

THE MINOAN CIVILIZATION was the earliest known civilization in Europe, dominating the Aegean Sea in the Mediterranean from about 2000 to 1450 B.C. The Minoans' homeland was the island of Crete, from which they traded as far afield as Egypt, Syria, and the Greek mainland. Minoan culture also had a powerful impact on other Aegean islands, such as Thera. The Minoans built elegant stone palaces, the largest of which was at Knossos in Crete. The palace walls were decorated with frescoes showing scenes of Minoan life, such as religious rituals. One fresco shows a ritual in which young men and women catch hold of a bull's horns and then leap over it. Bulls had religious importance and were often sacrificed. The Minoan religion included the worship of a mother goddess, who was sometimes depicted holding two snakes. In the 15th century B.C., a people from the Greek mainland, the Mycenaeans, took over Knossos and succeeded the Minoans as the dominant power in the Aegean. Mainland Greece was ruled by the Mycenaeans as a series of small kingdoms. These were governed from palaces that were often heavily fortified. The Mycenaeans copied the Minoan art of fresco painting, and adapted Minoan writing to fit their own language. Their pottery and metalwork also showed Minoan influence.

Dog   Snake   Dog

Gold
disk

Owl   Monkey

**FRESCO SHOWING BULL-LEAPERS
FROM KNOSSOS, CRETE**

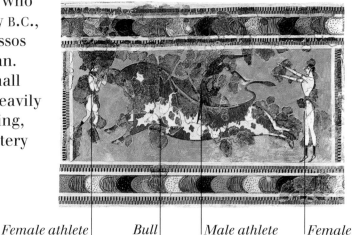

Female athlete
grasping the
bull's horns

Bull

Male athlete
leaping over
the bull's back

Female
athlete

**SIDE VIEW OF A PAINTED STONE SARCOPHAGUS
FROM AYIA TRIADA, CRETE**

Double-headed ax,
a sacred symbol

Woman emptying vessel

Man carrying
boat

Bird

Man playing lyre

Sacred tree

Figure dressed
in animal skin

Tomb

Altar

Woman
carrying
vessels

Men carrying
animals

Column

Vessel

FIGURINE OF THE MOTHER GODDESS

Bird

Tiara

Snake

Bodice

Apron

Flounced
skirt

FRESCO FROM A MINOAN SETTLEMENT ON THERA

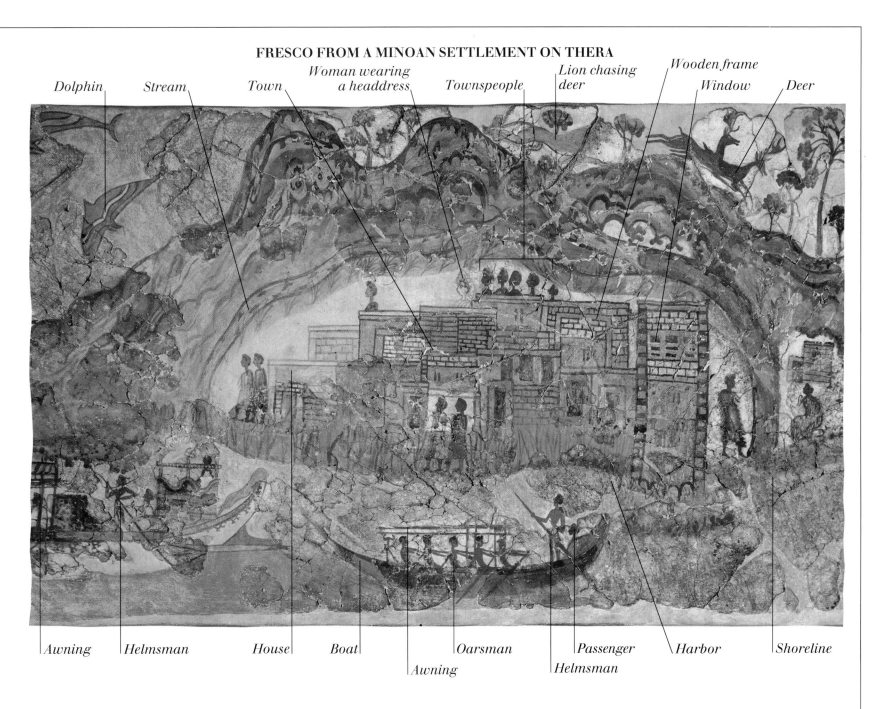

Dolphin   Stream   Town   Woman wearing a headdress   Townspeople   Lion chasing deer   Wooden frame   Window   Deer

Awning   Helmsman   House   Boat   Awning   Oarsman   Passenger   Helmsman   Harbor   Shoreline

GOLD DEATH MASK FROM A TOMB AT MYCENAE

POTTERY JAR FROM A MYCENAEAN COLONY ON RHODES

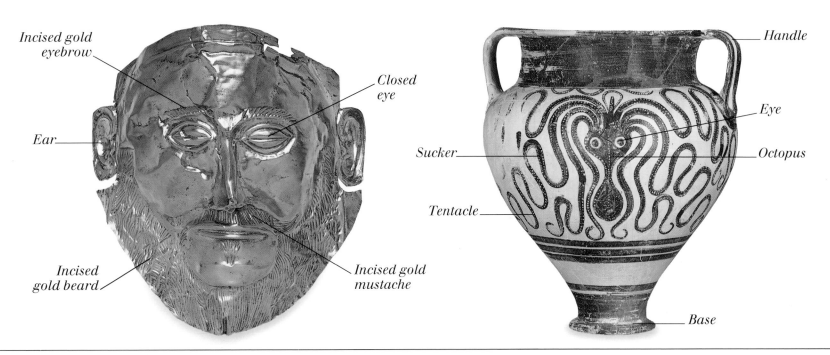

Incised gold eyebrow   Closed eye   Ear   Incised gold beard   Incised gold mustache

Handle   Eye   Sucker   Octopus   Tentacle   Base

Greece: architecture

THE GREATEST PERIOD OF GREEK CIVILIZATION lasted from about the eighth century until the fourth century B.C. Ancient Greece was not a unified country, but a collection of city states, such as Athens and Sparta, that were linked by a common language and culture. Elegant and well-proportioned architecture was created throughout the Greek world. There were three main architectural styles, known as orders. These were the Doric, Ionic, and Corinthian orders, chiefly distinguished by the types of stone capitals at the top of a building's columns. Doric capitals were simple and sturdy; Ionic capitals had spiral scrolls called volutes; and Corinthian capitals were adorned with carved acanthus leaves. Columns were occasionally replaced by load-bearing statues known as caryatids. The example shown here is from a temple on the Acropolis (citadel) of Athens, which was also the religious center of the city. The architectural styles were also used by Greek colonists overseas, and one of the best preserved Greek temples is the Doric temple of Hera at Paestum in Italy. Greek cultural influences also spread to other groups, such as the Lycians of southern Turkey, whose rulers built their tombs in the form of Greek temples.

HORSE'S HEAD FROM
THE ACROPOLIS, ATHENS

Doric
capital

Female
figure

Draped
robe

Base

CARYATID FROM
THE ACROPOLIS, ATHENS

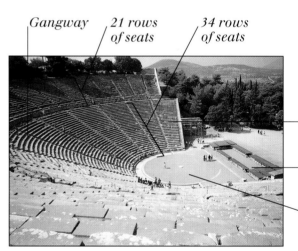

Gangway

21 rows
of seats

34 rows
of seats

14,000-seat auditorium
cut into the hillside

Area of skene (stage
backdrop and dressing-room)

Acting area

THEATER, EPIDAUROS, GREECE

TEMPLE OF HERA, PAESTUM, ITALY

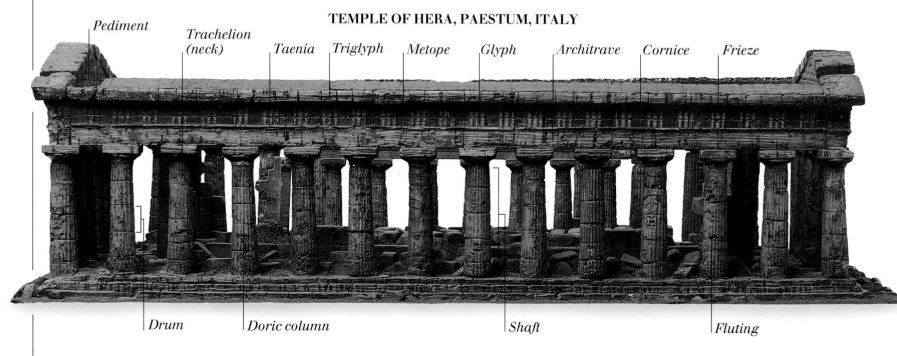

Pediment

Trachelion
(neck)

Taenia

Triglyph

Metope

Glyph

Architrave

Cornice

Frieze

Drum

Doric column

Shaft

Fluting

CAPITALS OF THE THREE ORDERS OF GREEK ARCHITECTURE

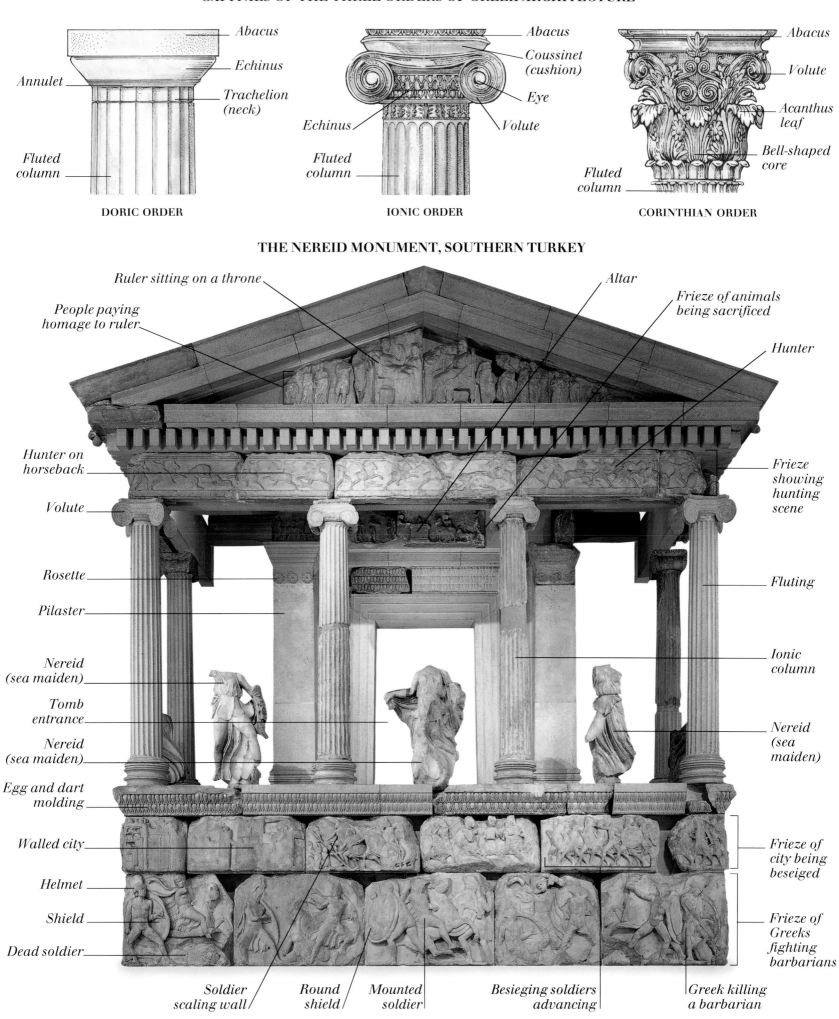

Abacus

Echinus

Annulet

Trachelion (neck)

Fluted column

DORIC ORDER

Abacus

Coussinet (cushion)

Eye

Volute

Echinus

Fluted column

IONIC ORDER

Abacus

Volute

Acanthus leaf

Bell-shaped core

Fluted column

CORINTHIAN ORDER

THE NEREID MONUMENT, SOUTHERN TURKEY

Ruler sitting on a throne

People paying homage to ruler

Altar

Frieze of animals being sacrificed

Hunter

Hunter on horseback

Frieze showing hunting scene

Volute

Rosette

Fluting

Pilaster

Nereid (sea maiden)

Ionic column

Tomb entrance

Nereid (sea maiden)

Nereid (sea maiden)

Egg and dart molding

Walled city

Frieze of city being beseiged

Helmet

Shield

Frieze of Greeks fighting barbarians

Dead soldier

Soldier scaling wall

Round shield

Mounted soldier

Besieging soldiers advancing

Greek killing a barbarian

27

Greece: mythology

THE GREEKS BELIEVED in many deities, mythological creatures, and human heroes. The main gods and goddesses were related to one another and lived, with the god Zeus as their king, on top of Mount Olympus, in western Greece. Each deity had his or her own sphere of influence; Aphrodite, for instance, was the goddess of love and beauty, and Poseidon was god of the sea. Stories or myths about the adventures of gods and goddesses often involved legendary human heroes, such as Odysseus. He was a Greek warrior who took part in the siege of the city of Troy, and in his travels home encountered many dangers, such as the sirens, mythological creatures that tried to lure sailors to their death. One of the most famous Greek heroes was Herakles, who is depicted on friezes from the temple at Bassae fighting a race of warrior women, the Amazons. Another section of the same frieze shows creatures called centaurs, who were part human and part horse, at the wedding feast of the king of a Greek people known as the Lapiths. The centaurs drank too much wine, tried to carry off the Lapith women, and so provoked a fight.

STATUE OF ZEUS, KING OF THE GODS

MIRROR CASE SHOWING DEITIES PLAYING A GAME OF KNUCKLEBONES

Eros, son of Aphrodite

Pan, god of the countryside

Goat's leg

Knucklebones

Aphrodite, goddess of love and beauty

Goose, associated with Aphrodite

FRIEZE SHOWING GREEKS AND AMAZONS FIGHTING FROM THE TEMPLE AT BASSAE, GREECE

Herakles

Amazon

Greek pulling Amazon from horse

Horse trampling a Greek

Amazon

Fallen Greek

Hippolyte, an Amazon

Lion skin

Fallen horse

KYLIX (DRINKING CUP) SHOWING POSEIDON

Handle

Fish tail

Poseidon, god of the sea

Horse's head

Trident

Eye

Base

Hippocampus, a sea-monster

STAMNOS (STORAGE JAR) SHOWING ODYSSEUS AND THE SIRENS

Siren, a singing sea-nymph part woman and part bird

Siren calling sailors to death on rocks

Rock

Ophthalmos (eye)

Odysseus strapped to the mast to prevent him from obeying the sirens

Kubernetes (helmsman)

Sailors with ears blocked to prevent them from hearing the sirens

Pedalia (twin rudder)

Kope (oar)

Thyrsus (rod entwined with vines or ivy)

Aphrodite

Dionysus

Poseidon

Trident

Bride

Artemis

Lyre

Rosette

Bridegroom

Hermes

Apollo

Bridle

Chariot

Rein

Harpy

Chariot wheel

Horse

AMPHORA (STORAGE JAR) SHOWING GODS AND GODDESSES IN A BRIDAL PROCESSION

FRIEZE SHOWING LAPITHS AND CENTAURS FIGHTING, FROM THE TEMPLE AT BASSAE, GREECE

Lapith woman clutching statue

Lapith youth attacking centaur

Centaur, a creature part human and part horse

Lapith woman seeking refuge at a shrine

Statue of goddess

Centaur pulling robe

Panther skin hanging on a tree, indicating a sacred grave

Greece: everyday life

DOLPHIN-SHAPED OIL CONTAINER

MOST GREEKS LIVED in city states, such as Athens and Sparta, which consisted of the city and its surrounding countryside. Country houses were usually built around a courtyard, and many rooms were designed for specific functions. The andron was a dining room used by the men of the house for entertaining their male friends. Women had separate quarters, called the gynaeceum, where they spent some of their time preparing wool and weaving. Special items were used for making textiles; an epinetron, for example, was a protective leg shield that was sometimes worn over the knee and thigh of a seated woman. Greek farmers produced a variety of crops, such as barley, wheat, and grapes, as well as olives, which were knocked down from trees with long sticks. Grapes were made into wine that was drunk at symposia, which were dining and drinking parties for men. At a symposium, men reclined on couches and drank from special vessels, such as a shallow cup called a kylix, or a cup shaped like a horn or animal's head, called a rhyton. As the men joked and discussed politics or philosophy, slave girls waited on and entertained them by dancing or playing musical instruments.

Man knocking olives out of tree

Handle

Olive tree

Falling olive

Man shaking branch with stick

Man collecting olives

VASE SHOWING AN OLIVE HARVEST

A GREEK FARMHOUSE

Ladder to upper story

Gynaeceum (women's quarters)

Courtyard

Brick wall with plaster

Terracotta tile

Andron (dining room for men)

Household altar

Wooden shutter

Hearth

Porch pillar

Stone wall

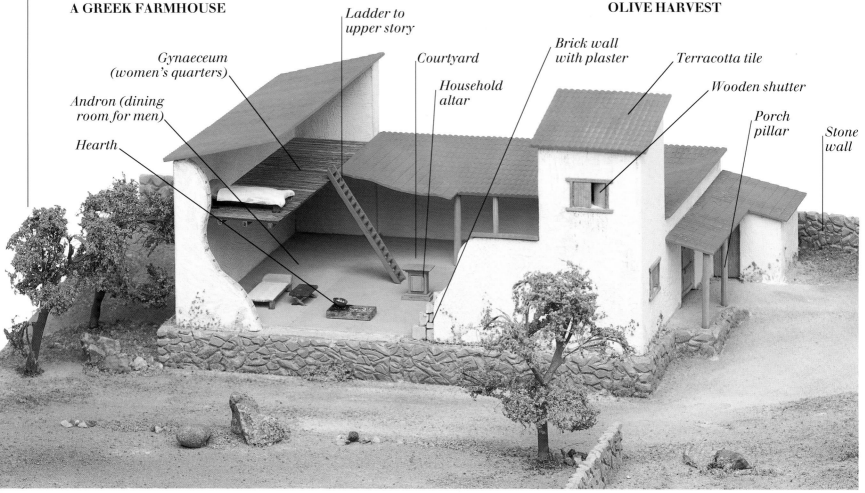

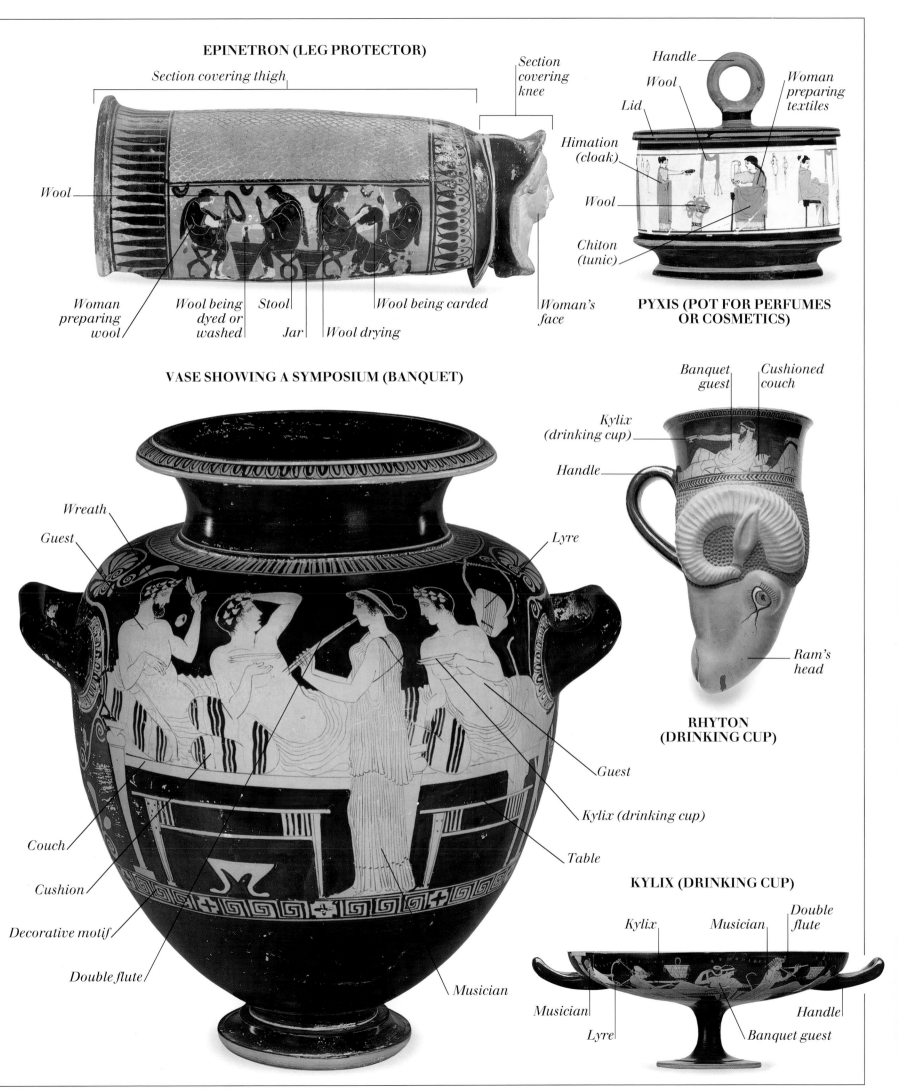

EPINETRON (LEG PROTECTOR)

Section covering thigh

Section covering knee

Wool

Woman preparing wool

Wool being dyed or washed

Stool

Jar

Wool drying

Wool being carded

Woman's face

PYXIS (POT FOR PERFUMES OR COSMETICS)

Handle

Wool

Lid

Woman preparing textiles

Himation (cloak)

Wool

Chiton (tunic)

VASE SHOWING A SYMPOSIUM (BANQUET)

Wreath

Guest

Lyre

Guest

Kylix (drinking cup)

Table

Couch

Cushion

Decorative motif

Double flute

Musician

RHYTON (DRINKING CUP)

Banquet guest

Cushioned couch

Kylix (drinking cup)

Handle

Ram's head

KYLIX (DRINKING CUP)

Kylix

Musician

Double flute

Musician

Lyre

Handle

Banquet guest

31

Rome: the army

ROME WAS ONE OF A NUMBER of towns under Etruscan influence until 509 B.C., when the Romans overthrew their kings and established a republic. Over the following centuries, Rome expanded to become the dominant power in the Mediterranean region. In 27 B.C., after a period of unrest and civil war, Augustus became the first Roman emperor. He restored peace and for the next 450 years Rome and its vast territories were governed by emperors. Rome's success was founded on its well-organized army. The army was divided into legions of 5,000 soldiers, who were called legionaries. A legion consisted of ten cohorts, each with six centuries consisting of about 80 men. The legions were backed up by auxiliary troops—cavalry and infantry units often composed of non-Roman citizens. A legionary's armor included a helmet and a cuirass that protected the upper body. A legionary's usual weapons were a spear, a short sword, and a dagger. The Romans celebrated their military successes with parades and depicted them in sculptured reliefs. For example, reliefs showing the conquest of Romania, then called Dacia, adorn Trajan's column in Rome.

HORSEHEAD ARMOR

IMPERIAL GALLIC HELMET

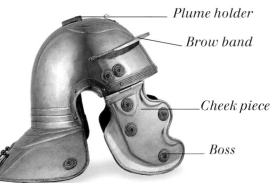

Plume holder

Brow band

Cheek piece

Boss

CUIRASS (LORICA SEGMENTATA)

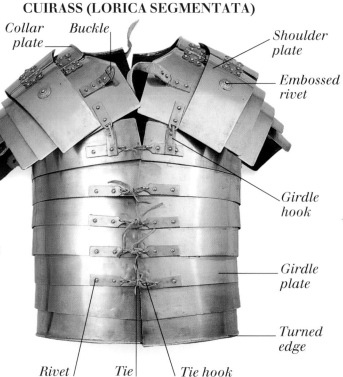

Collar plate

Buckle

Shoulder plate

Embossed rivet

Girdle hook

Girdle plate

Turned edge

Rivet

Tie

Tie hook

SWORD AND SCABBARD

Emperor Tiberius receiving his nephew Germanicus

Portrait of Emperor Tiberius

Shrine

Legion's eagle standard

Blade

RELIEF FROM THE BASE OF THE COLUMN OF ANTONINUS PIUS SHOWING A CAVALRY PARADE

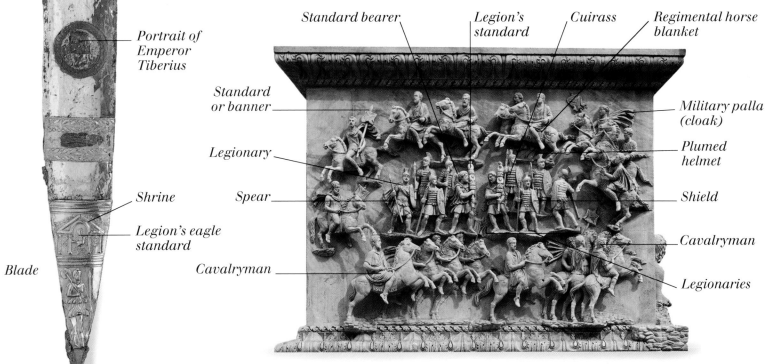

Standard bearer

Legion's standard

Cuirass

Regimental horse blanket

Standard or banner

Legionary

Spear

Cavalryman

Military palla (cloak)

Plumed helmet

Shield

Cavalryman

Legionaries

SECTION OF TRAJAN'S COLUMN SHOWING SCENES FROM THE CAMPAIGN AGAINST DACIA

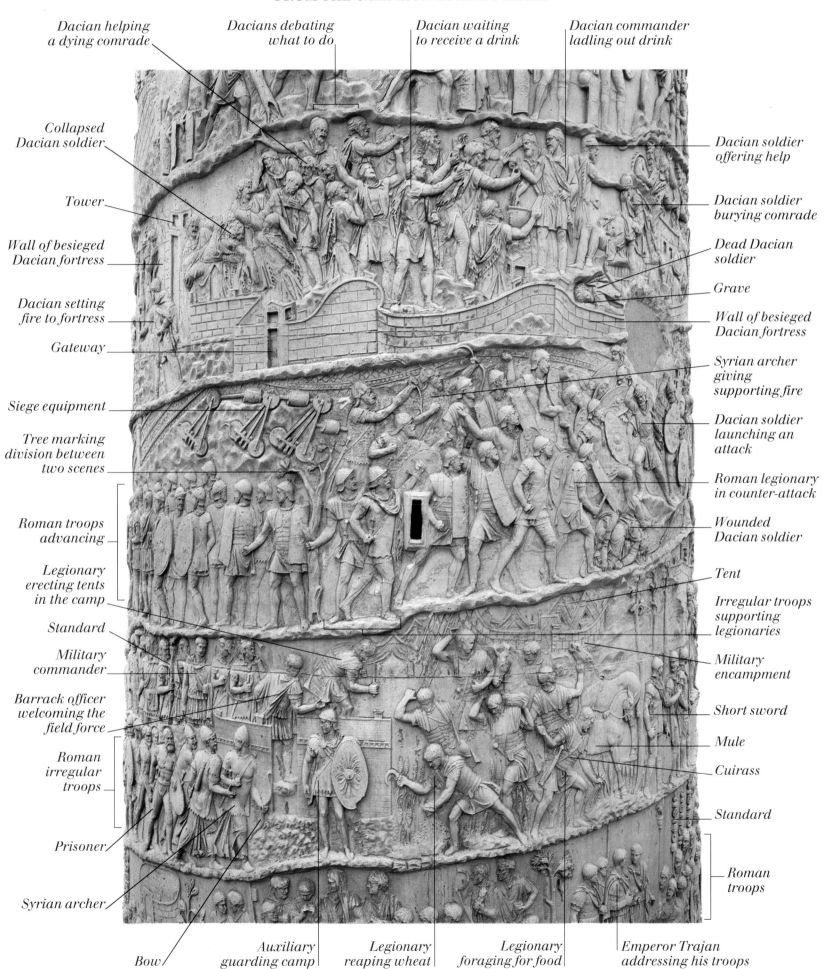

Dacian helping a dying comrade

Dacians debating what to do

Dacian waiting to receive a drink

Dacian commander ladling out drink

Collapsed Dacian soldier

Dacian soldier offering help

Tower

Dacian soldier burying comrade

Wall of besieged Dacian fortress

Dead Dacian soldier

Dacian setting fire to fortress

Grave

Gateway

Wall of besieged Dacian fortress

Siege equipment

Syrian archer giving supporting fire

Tree marking division between two scenes

Dacian soldier launching an attack

Roman troops advancing

Roman legionary in counter-attack

Legionary erecting tents in the camp

Wounded Dacian soldier

Tent

Irregular troops supporting legionaries

Standard

Military commander

Military encampment

Barrack officer welcoming the field force

Short sword

Roman irregular troops

Mule

Cuirass

Standard

Prisoner

Roman troops

Syrian archer

Bow

Auxiliary guarding camp

Legionary reaping wheat

Legionary foraging for food

Emperor Trajan addressing his troops

Rome: architecture

LIBRARY OF CELSUS, EPHESUS, TURKEY

Bʏ ᴛʜᴇ ꜰɪʀsᴛ ᴄᴇɴᴛᴜʀʏ, Rome had become the largest city in the western world, with more than a million inhabitants. The city steadily acquired an array of magnificent civic buildings—temples, stadiums, and public baths—designed to reflect the might of the Roman Empire. Two of the most impressive monuments in Rome were the Colosseum, a huge amphitheater seating 50,000 people; and the Pantheon, a temple that had the largest dome in the world at the time. Both of these monuments were partly built in concrete, an often-used Roman building material, and they had typical Roman architectural features. The Colosseum had decorative columns and arches, and the Pantheon had a massive dome and an elaborate, marble-veneered interior. The Romans built extensively throughout their empire, which extended from the Atlantic Ocean past the Black Sea at its greatest extent. They laid out new cities on a grid plan, and constructed aqueducts—water channels raised on arches in some places—to provide them with a water supply. By the third century, most cities were defended by walls with fortified gateways, of which the Porta Nigra is an example.

MAP OF ANCIENT ROME

- Stadium of Domitian
- Pantheon
- Gardens of Lucullus
- Camp of the Praetorian Guard
- Forum of Trajan
- Forum Romanum
- Aqueduct
- Baths of Trajan
- Colosseum
- Imperial palace
- Circus Maximus
- Baths of Caracalla
- Tiber River

PORTA NIGRA, TRIER, GERMANY, c.180

- Semicircular tower lacking original top story
- Parapet
- Round-arched window
- Semicircular tower
- Crowning cornice
- Pilaster
- Keystone
- Frieze
- Entablature
- Shaft
- Attached column
- Lobby
- Round arch
- Entrance to town
- Capital
- Base

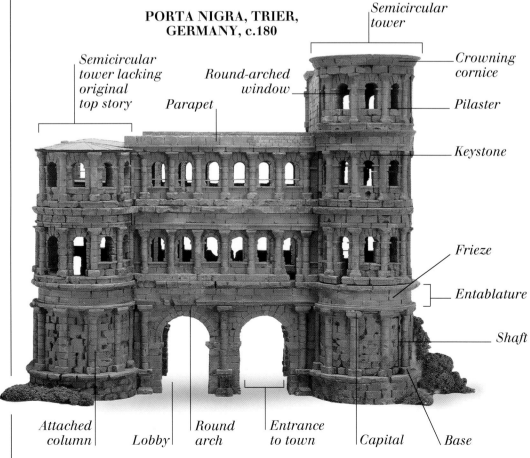

- Crowning cornice
- Velarium (bracket for awning)
- Pilaster
- Fourth floor
- Entablature
- Corinthian half-column
- Third floor
- Ionic half-column
- Second floor
- Doric half-column
- First floor

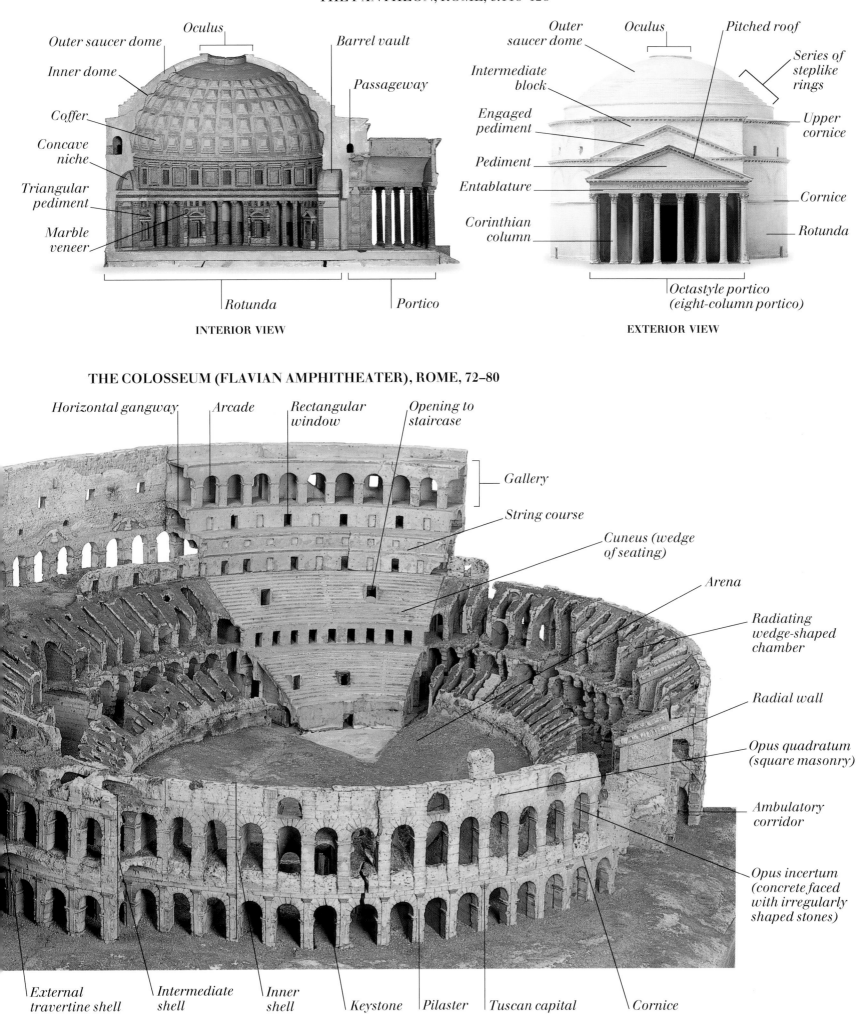

THE PANTHEON, ROME, c.118–128

INTERIOR VIEW

Outer saucer dome
Oculus
Inner dome
Barrel vault
Passageway
Coffer
Concave niche
Triangular pediment
Marble veneer
Rotunda
Portico

EXTERIOR VIEW

Outer saucer dome
Oculus
Pitched roof
Series of steplike rings
Intermediate block
Engaged pediment
Upper cornice
Pediment
Entablature
Corinthian column
Cornice
Rotunda
Octastyle portico (eight-column portico)

THE COLOSSEUM (FLAVIAN AMPHITHEATER), ROME, 72–80

Horizontal gangway
Arcade
Rectangular window
Opening to staircase
Gallery
String course
Cuneus (wedge of seating)
Arena
Radiating wedge-shaped chamber
Radial wall
Opus quadratum (square masonry)
Ambulatory corridor
Opus incertum (concrete faced with irregularly shaped stones)
External travertine shell
Intermediate shell
Inner shell
Keystone
Pilaster
Tuscan capital
Cornice

35

Rome: imperial trade and prosperity

THE ROMAN EMPIRE created conditions that allowed trade and prosperity to grow in the Mediterranean region and much of Europe. The empire imposed stability on the area, removed internal barriers to trade, and created both a single currency and standard weights and measures. Rome itself was the hub of the trade network: like all the large cities of the empire, it was obliged to import food, most notably grain from Egypt and North Africa. More exotic imports included wild animals from Britain, Germany, and the Near East (for the circus), and silks and spices from the Far East. In return, artisans in Rome produced jewelry, fine pots, and bronze jugs to be sold abroad. The most economical means of transport for trade goods was by ship, across the sea and along the great rivers, such as the Rhine. Wine, olive oil, and fish paste were transported in pottery storage jars called amphorae, which could be packed tightly in the hold of a ship. As settlements and military camps developed in different provinces of the empire, the Roman way of life spread, creating an increased demand for Roman goods such as wine, fine pottery, and glass. In time, cities and regions outside Rome began to produce their own goods; Cologne in Germany, for example, became famous for its glassware.

GOLD EARRINGS

CAMEO SHOWING EMPEROR AUGUSTUS

Jeweled crown (added later)

Sardonyx

Carved white onyx

Aegis of Minerva

EXAMPLES OF ROMAN COINS

Laurel crown

As, the smallest bronze coin

Head of emperor

Aureus, gold coin worth 100 sestertii

Sestertius, bronze coin worth four asses

Denarius, silver coin worth 16 asses

BRONZE STEELYARD AND WEIGHT

Hook for hanging the steelyard

Arm inscribed with scale

Acorn-shaped weight

Hook for weighing objects in bags

STONE RELIEF SHOWING SHOP SCENE

Embroidered material

Cover

Cushion

Tiled roof

Corinthian column

Shop assistant

Shopkeeper

Attendants

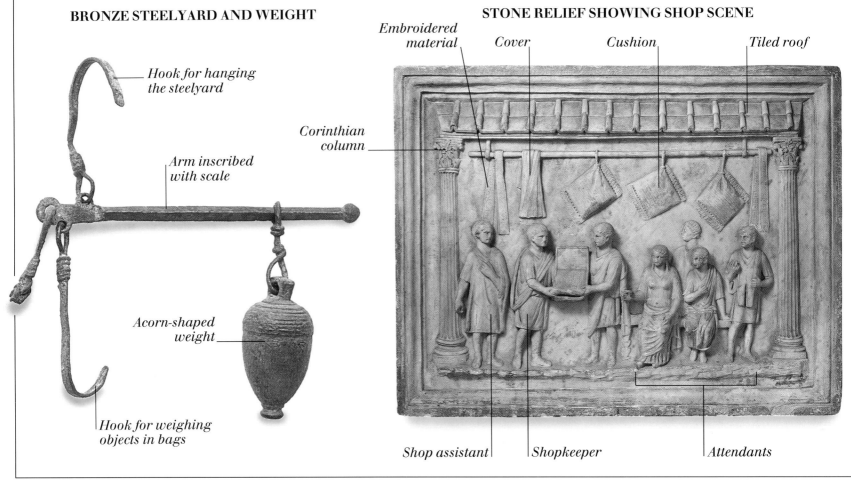

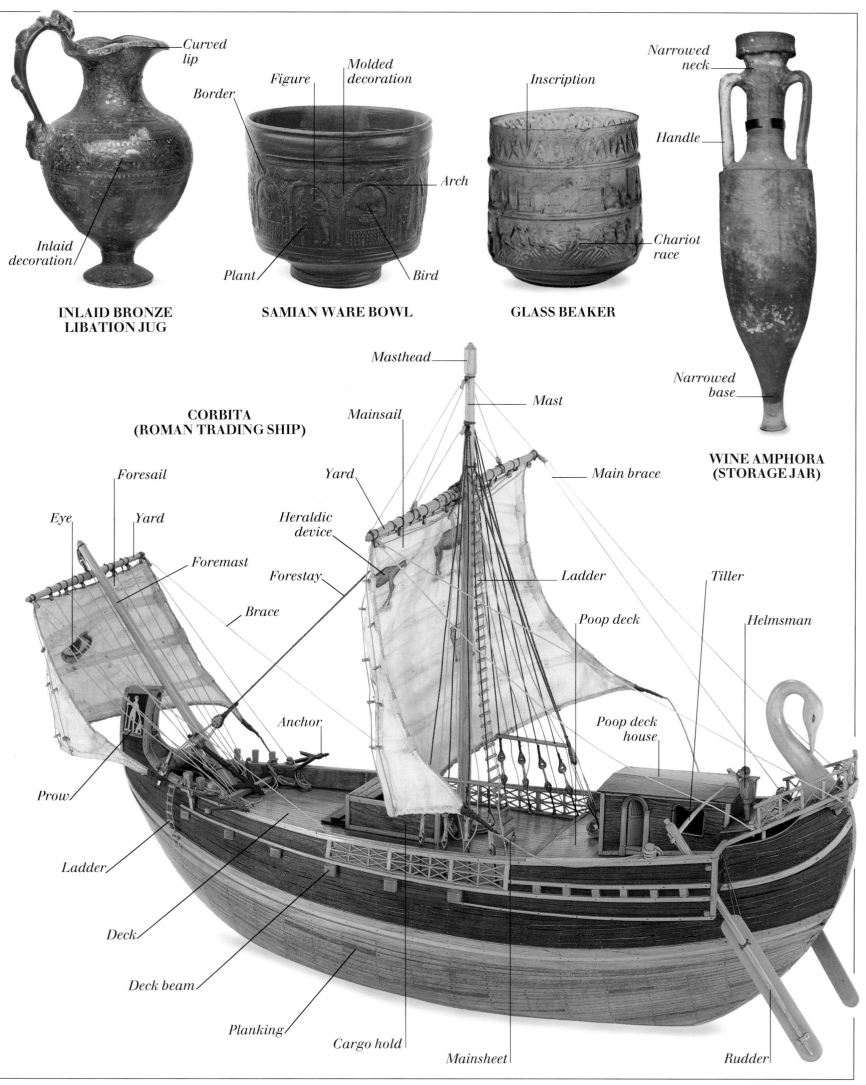

Curved lip

Border

Figure

Molded decoration

Inscription

Narrowed neck

Handle

Arch

Inlaid decoration

Plant

Bird

Chariot race

**INLAID BRONZE
LIBATION JUG**

SAMIAN WARE BOWL

GLASS BEAKER

Narrowed base

**WINE AMPHORA
(STORAGE JAR)**

Masthead

Mast

**CORBITA
(ROMAN TRADING SHIP)**

Mainsail

Yard

Main brace

Foresail

Eye

Yard

Heraldic device

Ladder

Tiller

Foremast

Forestay

Helmsman

Brace

Poop deck

Anchor

Poop deck house

Prow

Ladder

Deck

Deck beam

Planking

Cargo hold

Mainsheet

Rudder

The Maya

THE MAYAN CIVILIZATION was one of the major civilizations of the ancient Americas. Reaching its height between about 250 and 900, this sophisticated civilization spread across much of Central America. There, great Mayan cities were dominated by stone palaces and by temple-topped, stepped pyramids. Mayan society was hierarchically organized, and the ruler and other important people, such as nobles and warriors, wore colorful feathered headdresses that distinguished them from the rest of the population. Mayan life was dominated by deities that were linked with aspects of the natural world, such as the Sun, Moon, and rain. The daily "death" of the Sun at nightfall and its "rebirth" at daybreak were reenacted in a symbolic battle called the ballgame, in which two teams propelled a hard rubber ball around a special court without using their hands and feet. The losing team was often put to death. Human sacrifice and other bloodletting rituals were important to the Maya, who believed that the gods required human blood for sustenance. The Maya were expert astronomers and mathematicians, and devised a complex calendar. They also used a representational form of writing made up of pictographic symbols known as glyphs.

BALL-COURT MARKER

VESSEL DECORATION SHOWING THE BALLGAME

Yoke for hitting ball | Ballgame player | Hummingbird headdress | Glyph | Ballgame player

Protection for one foot | Protection for one arm | Rubber ball | Black body paint | Protection for one knee

Padded clothing

POTTERY FIGURINES

Feather plume

Headdress

Ear flare

Jade necklace

Masquette

Jade bracelet

Decorated sandal

Headdress with serpent design

Serpent's eye

Serpent's fang

Serpent's jaw

Ear flare

Long, tapered nose

Fang

Vessel

Pectoral

Red body paint

Blue body paint

Flame

Ball of incense

Helmet

Ear flare

Protective armband

Yoke for hitting ball

Padded clothing

Sandal

BALLGAME PLAYER

NOBLEMAN

CHAC, GOD OF RAIN

LINTEL FROM CITY OF YAXCHILAN SHOWING BLOODLETTING RITE

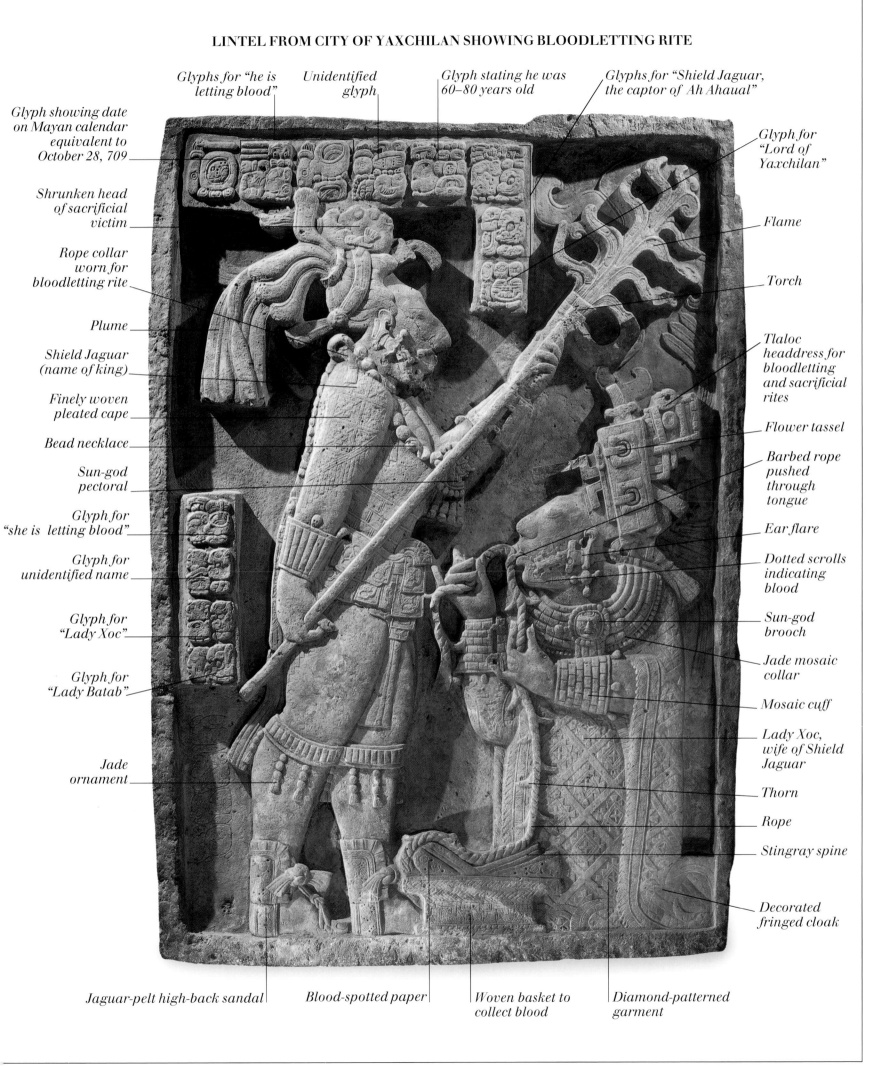

Glyphs for "he is letting blood"

Unidentified glyph

Glyph stating he was 60–80 years old

Glyphs for "Shield Jaguar, the captor of Ah Ahaual"

Glyph showing date on Mayan calendar equivalent to October 28, 709

Glyph for "Lord of Yaxchilan"

Shrunken head of sacrificial victim

Flame

Rope collar worn for bloodletting rite

Torch

Plume

Tlaloc headdress for bloodletting and sacrificial rites

Shield Jaguar (name of king)

Finely woven pleated cape

Flower tassel

Bead necklace

Barbed rope pushed through tongue

Sun-god pectoral

Glyph for "she is letting blood"

Ear flare

Glyph for unidentified name

Dotted scrolls indicating blood

Glyph for "Lady Xoc"

Sun-god brooch

Jade mosaic collar

Glyph for "Lady Batab"

Mosaic cuff

Lady Xoc, wife of Shield Jaguar

Jade ornament

Thorn

Rope

Stingray spine

Decorated fringed cloak

Jaguar-pelt high-back sandal

Blood-spotted paper

Woven basket to collect blood

Diamond-patterned garment

The Aztecs

STATUE OF XIPE TOTEC, GOD OF SPRINGTIME

DURING THE 15TH CENTURY, the Aztecs came to dominate large parts of Mexico, until they in turn were conquered by the Spaniards in 1521. Military prowess was important in the Aztec state, whose self-styled Warriors of the Sun waged wars to subjugate neighboring lands and to obtain tribute goods from them. Soldiers were rewarded with elaborate costumes to show how many captives they had taken, the most successful becoming Jaguar or Eagle Knights. The Aztec capital, Tenochtitlan, was built on a lake. At the center of the city was the Great Temple, built around older versions in onionlike layers, with a place of sacrifice at the top. Here some captives had their hearts cut out as offerings to the god Tlaloc and to sustain the god Huitzilopochtli in his daily battle to avert the end of the world—the Aztecs believed that they lived in the fifth and final world creation. Captives who were sacrificed to Xipe Totec, god of springtime, were skinned alive and priests then wore the victim's skin to symbolize renewal. The Aztecs were also expert astronomers, had a complex calendar system, and made beautiful manuscripts, such as the Codex Mendoza commissioned by the Spaniards.

AZTEC SUN STONE

4-Ehecatl, date of destruction of a previous world

Mask of earth monster or sun god

4-Ocelotl, date of destruction of a previous world

Claw

4-Atl, date of destruction of a previous world

Glyph for one day

4-Quiahuitl, date of destruction of a previous world

Band showing the 20 days of the Aztec month

Two confronting heads of Xiuhcoatl, the celestial serpent

GREAT TEMPLE AT TENOCHTITLAN

Temple of Huitzilopochtli, Aztec patron god

Frieze of human skulls

Temple of Tlaloc, god of rain

Sacrificial stone

Temple built c.1500

Incense burner

Temple built 1469

Temple built 1454

Temple built 1431

Chacmool figure, for holding the hearts of sacrificial victims

Temple built 1390

Steps down which victims' bodies were thrown

Brazier

Serpent head

Serpent head

Brazier

Possible nobles' or priests' residences

Stone showing the goddess Coyolxauhqui

Serpent head

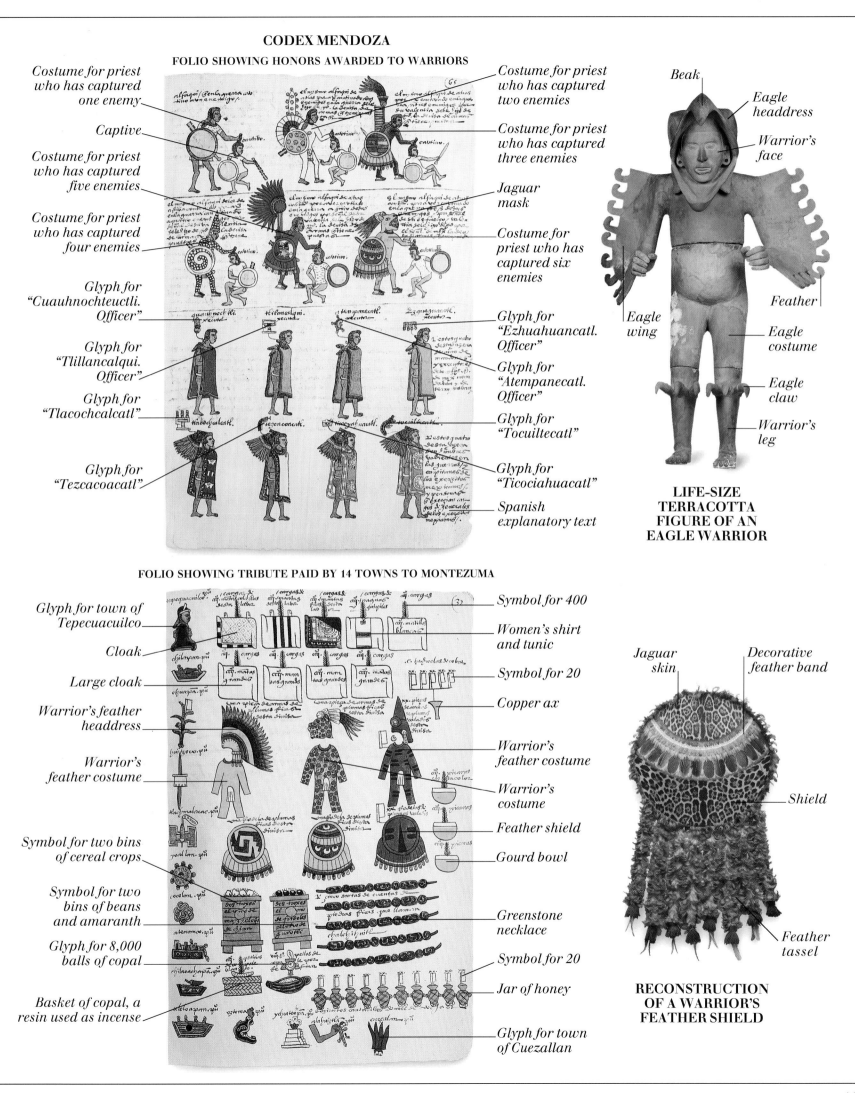

CODEX MENDOZA

FOLIO SHOWING HONORS AWARDED TO WARRIORS

- *Costume for priest who has captured one enemy*
- *Captive*
- *Costume for priest who has captured five enemies*
- *Costume for priest who has captured four enemies*
- *Glyph for "Cuauhnochteuctli. Officer"*
- *Glyph for "Tlillancalqui. Officer"*
- *Glyph for "Tlacochcalcatl"*
- *Glyph for "Tezcacoacatl"*

- *Costume for priest who has captured two enemies*
- *Costume for priest who has captured three enemies*
- *Jaguar mask*
- *Costume for priest who has captured six enemies*
- *Glyph for "Ezhuahuancatl. Officer"*
- *Glyph for "Atempanecatl. Officer"*
- *Glyph for "Tocuiltecatl"*
- *Glyph for "Ticociahuacatl"*
- *Spanish explanatory text*

FOLIO SHOWING TRIBUTE PAID BY 14 TOWNS TO MONTEZUMA

- *Glyph for town of Tepecuacuilco*
- *Cloak*
- *Large cloak*
- *Warrior's feather headdress*
- *Warrior's feather costume*
- *Symbol for two bins of cereal crops*
- *Symbol for two bins of beans and amaranth*
- *Glyph for 8,000 balls of copal*
- *Basket of copal, a resin used as incense*

- *Symbol for 400*
- *Women's shirt and tunic*
- *Symbol for 20*
- *Copper ax*
- *Warrior's feather costume*
- *Warrior's costume*
- *Feather shield*
- *Gourd bowl*
- *Greenstone necklace*
- *Symbol for 20*
- *Jar of honey*
- *Glyph for town of Cuezallan*

- *Beak*
- *Eagle headdress*
- *Warrior's face*
- *Eagle wing*
- *Feather*
- *Eagle costume*
- *Eagle claw*
- *Warrior's leg*

LIFE-SIZE TERRACOTTA FIGURE OF AN EAGLE WARRIOR

- *Jaguar skin*
- *Decorative feather band*
- *Shield*
- *Feather tassel*

RECONSTRUCTION OF A WARRIOR'S FEATHER SHIELD

Andean civilizations

INCA GOLD LLAMA

THE ANDES REGION OF SOUTH AMERICA—a long mountainous area running parallel to the Pacific Ocean—was inhabited by many civilizations, including the Moche, Chimu, and Inca. Although the Andean civilizations occupied different parts of the region at various periods from the 18th century B.C. until the 16th century A.D., they shared some characteristics. Common aspects included crafts, such as elaborate goldwork, pottery, and textiles; the use of the llama as a beast of burden and a source of wool and meat; well-trained armies; similar beliefs and deities, such as a Sun and jaguar god; a reverence for mountaintops; and the practice of human sacrifice. The Moche, famed for their pottery, flourished during the first six centuries A.D. They were also skilled engineers and built a network of roads over mountainous terrain that gave them good control over their subject territories. The Chimu, who were famed for their goldwork, ruled northern Peru from about 800 until their defeat by the Incas in 1476. The Incas built towns, bridges, and new roads, and used the skills of subject craftspeople to produce fine textiles and goldwork. The Inca Empire was the largest ever seen in the Andes, but it fell to the Spanish conquerors less than 100 years later.

INCA UNQO (TUNIC)

Checkered motif

Slit for neck

T'okapu band with important symbols

Patterns give information about the wearer

CHIMU GOLD DOUBLE-SPOUTED WATER POT

Crescent-shaped headdress

Ear ornament

Human face

Bridge handle

Crow-step pattern

Spout

Spout

Gold openwork

Stylized animal head

Deer

Patterned base

CHIMU TUMI (CEREMONIAL KNIFE) OF THE SKY OR MOON GOD

Crescent-shaped headdress

Gold and turquoise ear flare

Disk

Turquoise inlay

Blade

MOCHE POTTERY

POT SHOWING MOUNTAIN SCENE

God, possibly Ai Apec

Sacred mountain

Snake with ears, enemy of Ai Apec

Mountain peak

Ai Apec's assistant

Ai Apec's assistant

Warrior

Seated figure

Snake

Plant

Figure, possibly a sacrificial victim

Bird

POT SHOWING TWO FIGURES

Feline deity

Fang

Paw

Seated figure, possibly a prisoner

Claw

POT SHOWING MESSENGERS

Spout

Man beating a drum

Scene showing messengers running

WARRIOR-SHAPED POT

Helmet

Spiral-patterned shirt

Weapon

Shield

North American civilizations

IN SOUTHWESTERN NORTH AMERICA, three prehistoric civilizations—the Hohokam, the Mogollon, and the Anasazi—flourished between the first century and the 15th century. All three were influenced by the civilizations of Mexico. The Hohokam were skilled farmers who irrigated the plains of southern Arizona. They were the first people to develop a decorative technique that used cactus juice, a weak acid, to etch designs on shells. The Mogollon were based in the mountains of New Mexico, where they lived in pit-houses. They produced a distinctive pottery, known as Mimbres pottery, which was often ritually punctured, possibly to allow the spirit of the owner to escape the body at death. In about 1300 the Mogollon civilization was absorbed by the more sophisticated Anasazi civilization, which dominated the region where the states of Utah, Arizona, Colorado, and New Mexico meet. The Anasazis' great achievement was their pueblos—complex settlements composed of rows of adjoining rooms, often several stories high. The largest, Pueblo Bonito in Chaco Canyon, New Mexico, contained over 800 rooms. Other pueblos such as Mesa Verde were built under the canyon cliffs. Each pueblo had a number of kivas—half-underground circular chambers where the men of the community would meet and perform ceremonies. The network of roads radiating from Chaco Canyon suggests it was an important trading center.

HOHOKAM
ETCHED
SHELL

Topknot

Facial
decoration

Loincloth

**ANASAZI POTTERY
EFFIGY JAR**

Rain symbol

Painted
geometric
design

ANASAZI POT

Oldest section

Kiva

Terrace

Mud ceiling
supported
by beams

Doorway

Continuous perimeter
wall for defense

Arbor to
provide shade

Plaza

Entrance
to pueblo

Great kiva

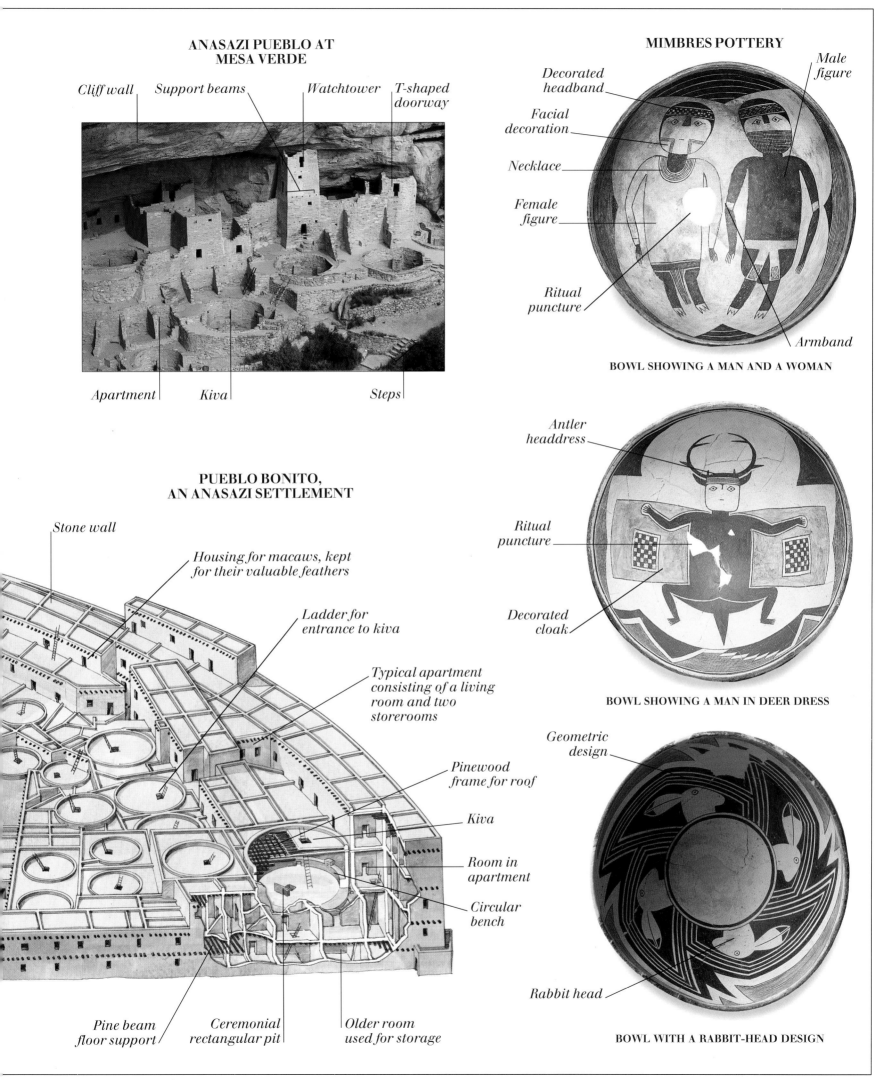

ANASAZI PUEBLO AT MESA VERDE

Cliff wall

Support beams

Watchtower

T-shaped doorway

Apartment

Kiva

Steps

PUEBLO BONITO, AN ANASAZI SETTLEMENT

Stone wall

Housing for macaws, kept for their valuable feathers

Ladder for entrance to kiva

Typical apartment consisting of a living room and two storerooms

Pinewood frame for roof

Kiva

Room in apartment

Circular bench

Pine beam floor support

Ceremonial rectangular pit

Older room used for storage

MIMBRES POTTERY

Decorated headband

Male figure

Facial decoration

Necklace

Female figure

Ritual puncture

Armband

BOWL SHOWING A MAN AND A WOMAN

Antler headdress

Ritual puncture

Decorated cloak

BOWL SHOWING A MAN IN DEER DRESS

Geometric design

Rabbit head

BOWL WITH A RABBIT-HEAD DESIGN

India: Buddhism

STATUE OF
THE BUDDHA

Tʜᴇ ʙᴜᴅᴅʜɪsᴛ ʀᴇʟɪɢɪᴏɴ was founded in northern India
about 2,500 years ago by a prince named Siddhartha Gautama.
He left his wife, family, and a luxurious palace for a life of
contemplation and wandering in search of spiritual truth.
After years spent exploring and considering different
spiritual paths, Siddhartha Gautama found enlightenment
while meditating under a pipal tree at Bodh Gaya. From
this time on, Siddhartha Gautama became known as
the Buddha, the Enlightened One. The Buddha was
a great spiritual teacher and when he died, in about
480 ʙ.ᴄ., his followers took his teachings to other parts of India.
Later, Buddhism reached southeastern Asia and the Far East,
and eventually became known throughout the world. The
Buddha's followers preserved ashes from his cremation as
relics and placed them in special containers called reliquaries.
These were often deposited in large moundlike structures
known as stupas. One of the great Buddhist stupas
was built at Amaravati in southern India. Reliefs
showing incidents from the life of the Buddha and
other Buddhist subjects covered the stupa and its
surrounding railing.

GOLD RELIQUARY

Garnet

Eagle

Ogee arch

Gesture of
fearlessness

Indra

The Buddha

Brahma

RELIEF FROM A STUPA,
NORTHERN INDIA

Auspicious
female figure

Guard

Reliquary

Table

Drona distributing
the Buddha's relics

THE STUPA AT AMARAVATI,
SOUTHERN INDIA

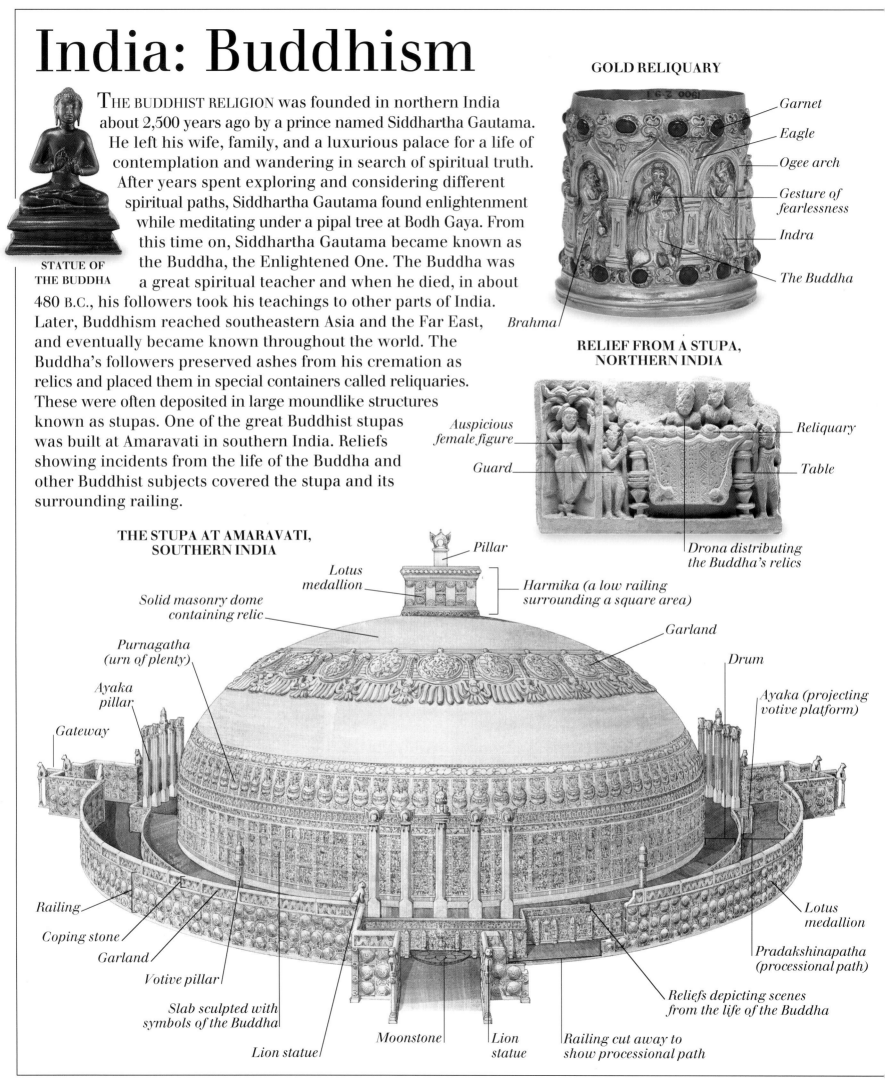

Pillar

Lotus
medallion

Solid masonry dome
containing relic

Harmika (a low railing
surrounding a square area)

Garland

Purnagatha
(urn of plenty)

Drum

Ayaka
pillar

Ayaka (projecting
votive platform)

Gateway

Railing

Coping stone

Garland

Votive pillar

Slab sculpted with
symbols of the Buddha

Lion statue

Moonstone

Lion
statue

Railing cut away to
show processional path

Reliefs depicting scenes
from the life of the Buddha

Pradakshinapatha
(processional path)

Lotus
medallion

FRIEZE FROM THE STUPA AT AMARAVATI SHOWING "THE GREAT DEPARTURE"

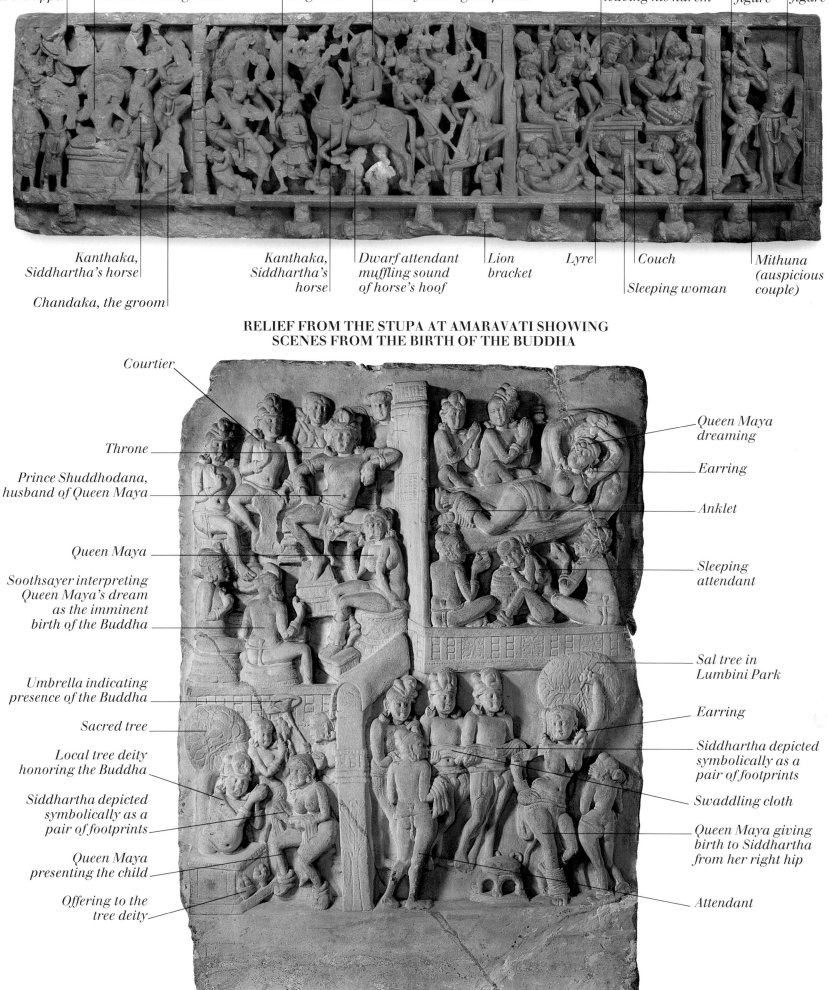

Celestial worshipper

Prince Siddhartha leaving his horse and groom

Chandaka, the groom

Prince Siddhartha secretly leaving his palace

Prince Siddhartha leaving his harem

Female figure

Male figure

Kanthaka, Siddhartha's horse

Chandaka, the groom

Kanthaka, Siddhartha's horse

Dwarf attendant muffling sound of horse's hoof

Lion bracket

Lyre

Couch

Sleeping woman

Mithuna (auspicious couple)

RELIEF FROM THE STUPA AT AMARAVATI SHOWING SCENES FROM THE BIRTH OF THE BUDDHA

Courtier

Throne

Prince Shuddhodana, husband of Queen Maya

Queen Maya

Soothsayer interpreting Queen Maya's dream as the imminent birth of the Buddha

Umbrella indicating presence of the Buddha

Sacred tree

Local tree deity honoring the Buddha

Siddhartha depicted symbolically as a pair of footprints

Queen Maya presenting the child

Offering to the tree deity

Queen Maya dreaming

Earring

Anklet

Sleeping attendant

Sal tree in Lumbini Park

Earring

Siddhartha depicted symbolically as a pair of footprints

Swaddling cloth

Queen Maya giving birth to Siddhartha from her right hip

Attendant

47

India: Hinduism

Oɴᴇ ᴏꜰ ᴛʜᴇ ᴍᴀᴊᴏʀ ʀᴇʟɪɢɪᴏɴꜱ of India, Hinduism, developed during the first thousand years A.D., although its origins are more ancient. Hinduism is a complex faith and its followers embrace a wide range of beliefs and practices. Most Hindus believe that at death the soul is reborn in another body, a process known as reincarnation. This continues until they finally gain release from the cycle of birth, death, and rebirth, by attaining a state called moksha. Hindus worship a large number of deities, including Shiva, an all-encompassing god, and his elephant-headed son Ganesha, and Vishnu, who is traditionally depicted in one of many incarnations or bodily forms. Female deities include Parvati, Shiva's wife, and Durga, a goddess who is famous for killing a demon in the form of a buffalo. Hindus often worship their deities in magnificent temple complexes built to traditional designs. The temple is the abode of a particular god or goddess, whose image is kept inside a central sanctuary. In major temples the sanctuary is usually surrounded by smaller shrines, and the entire complex is enclosed by a series of richly carved walls and gateways.

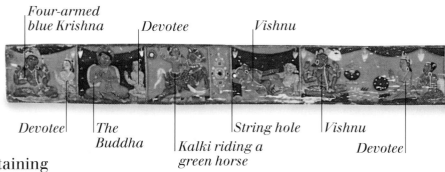

Four-armed blue Krishna   *Devotee*   *Vishnu*

Devotee   *The Buddha*   *Kalki riding a green horse*   *String hole*   *Vishnu*   *Devotee*

LION PILLAR FROM A TEMPLE

- *Lotus-petal capital*
- *Floral panel*
- *Pillar shaft*
- *Ear*
- *Lion*
- *Fang*
- *Mane*
- *Leg*
- *Paw*
- *Tail*
- *Pillar base*

IDEALIZED DEPICTION OF A TRADITIONAL HINDU TEMPLE

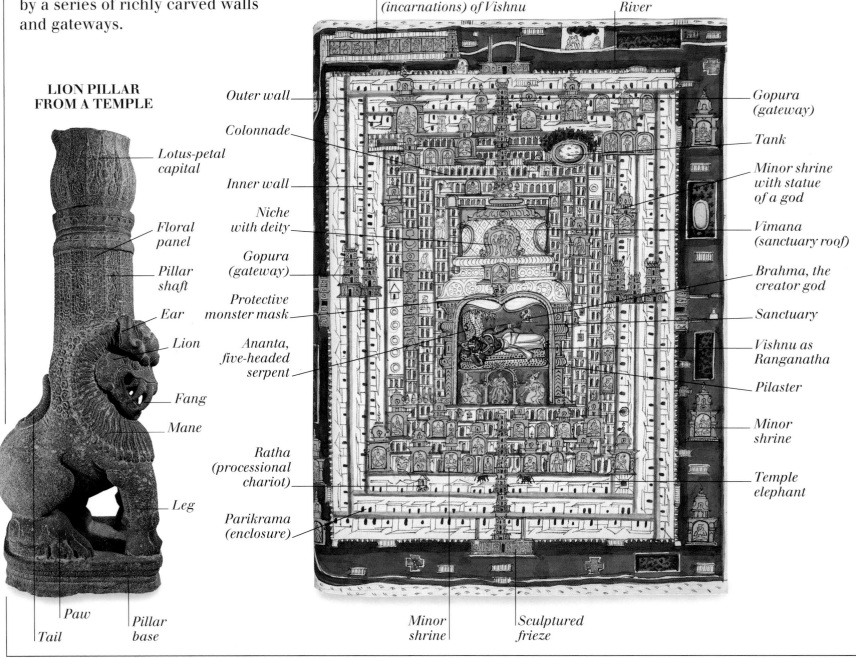

- *Shrine of the avataras (incarnations) of Vishnu*
- *River*
- *Outer wall*
- *Colonnade*
- *Inner wall*
- *Niche with deity*
- *Gopura (gateway)*
- *Protective monster mask*
- *Ananta, five-headed serpent*
- *Ratha (processional chariot)*
- *Parikrama (enclosure)*
- *Minor shrine*
- *Sculptured frieze*
- *Gopura (gateway)*
- *Tank*
- *Minor shrine with statue of a god*
- *Vimana (sanctuary roof)*
- *Brahma, the creator god*
- *Sanctuary*
- *Vishnu as Ranganatha*
- *Pilaster*
- *Minor shrine*
- *Temple elephant*

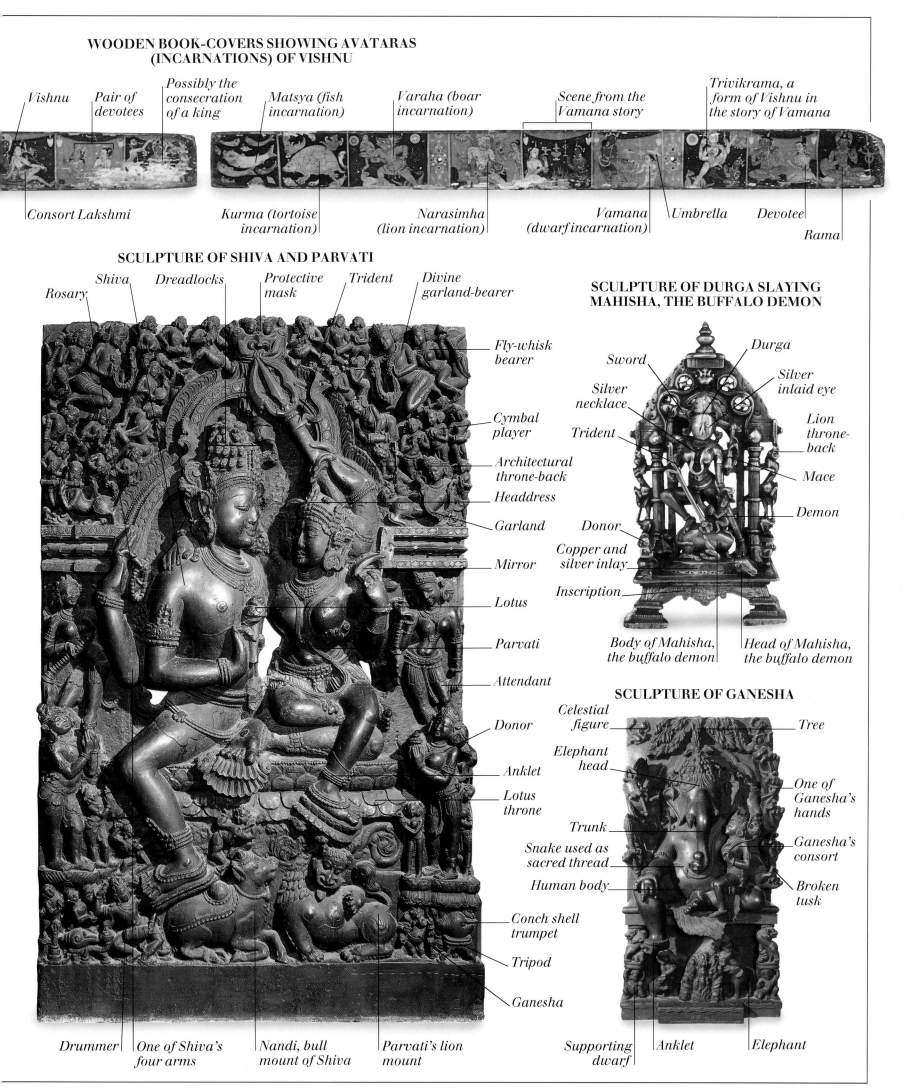

WOODEN BOOK-COVERS SHOWING AVATARAS (INCARNATIONS) OF VISHNU

Vishnu

Pair of devotees

Possibly the consecration of a king

Matsya (fish incarnation)

Varaha (boar incarnation)

Scene from the Vamana story

Trivikrama, a form of Vishnu in the story of Vamana

Consort Lakshmi

Kurma (tortoise incarnation)

Narasimha (lion incarnation)

Vamana (dwarf incarnation)

Umbrella

Devotee

Rama

SCULPTURE OF SHIVA AND PARVATI

Rosary

Shiva

Dreadlocks

Protective mask

Trident

Divine garland-bearer

Fly-whisk bearer

Cymbal player

Architectural throne-back

Headdress

Garland

Mirror

Lotus

Parvati

Attendant

Donor

Anklet

Lotus throne

Conch shell trumpet

Tripod

Ganesha

Drummer

One of Shiva's four arms

Nandi, bull mount of Shiva

Parvati's lion mount

SCULPTURE OF DURGA SLAYING MAHISHA, THE BUFFALO DEMON

Sword

Durga

Silver necklace

Silver inlaid eye

Trident

Lion throne-back

Mace

Demon

Donor

Copper and silver inlay

Inscription

Body of Mahisha, the buffalo demon

Head of Mahisha, the buffalo demon

SCULPTURE OF GANESHA

Celestial figure

Tree

Elephant head

One of Ganesha's hands

Trunk

Ganesha's consort

Snake used as sacred thread

Broken tusk

Human body

Supporting dwarf

Anklet

Elephant

49

China: everyday life

CHINA WAS A COLLECTION OF MANY KINGDOMS before it was united in 221 B.C. by the First Emperor of the Qin Dynasty, who created a strongly centralized state. The Han Dynasty took over from the Qin in 206 B.C., and ruled China for about 400 years. During this time, China experienced a period of peace and prosperity. Trade flourished as weights and measures were standardized and good trade routes were established across Asia to the west. The major Chinese export was silk, but merchants also traded bronze and iron utensils for horses, spices, and other goods. Han society was hierarchical; the emperor was the center of power, and there was a big difference between the living standards of the wealthy landowners and state officials, and the ordinary people. The Han developed a highly organized bureaucracy to administer the empire, which was large in terms of both geographical size and population. The cities were the administrative centers. Chinese imperial cities were laid out according to a rigid plan. The various districts were separated from each other by walls and gatehouses. Watchtowers were a popular feature of Chinese cities. The wealthy lived in mansions built around central courtyards, while the poor lived in simple buildings with walls of pounded earth. Han nobles enjoyed luxurious lives, as is shown by the array of objects found in their tombs, such as lacquerware and silks.

Cloud scroll

Decorated edge

Auspicious inscription

LACQUERWARE BOWL

Lidded cup

Chopstick

Wine cup | Tray | Food remains | Bowl

LACQUERWARE SET AND TRAY

Finial

Man keeping watch

Decorated eave tile

Dragon-headed bracket arm

Man

Tiled roof

Moat

Fish

TOMB MODEL OF A WATCHTOWER

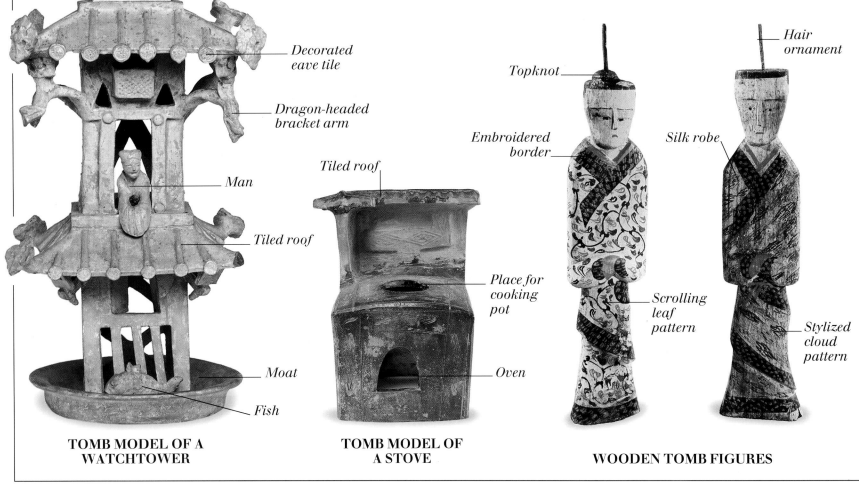

Tiled roof

Place for cooking pot

Oven

TOMB MODEL OF A STOVE

Topknot

Embroidered border

Scrolling leaf pattern

Hair ornament

Silk robe

Stylized cloud pattern

WOODEN TOMB FIGURES

CERAMIC MODEL OF A GATEHOUSE

Ridge of roof

Stamp showing a monster mask and ring

Carved flight of stairs

Tiled roof

Balcony railing

Stamp showing a horse and chariot

Window

Stamp showing an archer on horseback

Tiled roof

Bracket arm

Stamp showing a tree

Lintel

Stamp of a circle

Carved doorpost

Carved flight of stairs

Scroll pattern

Door guard

Halberd

Door guard

Stamp showing a building complex

Halberd

Stamp showing an archer on horseback

China: ritual and ceremony

THE ANCIENT CHINESE performed a range of religious rituals and ceremonies. The importance of various beliefs changed over time. During the Shang dynasty (c.1600–1027 B.C.), the Chinese worshipped ancestral spirits by making offerings of wine and food in magnificent bronze vessels. They also practiced human sacrifice. Shang diviners used animal bones, known as "oracle bones," to consult the spirits. Bones were heated until cracks appeared, from which the diviners interpreted the spirits' response to questions. The divinations were recorded on the bones, and are among the earliest examples of Chinese writing. The Zhou rulers, who overthrew the Shang in 1027 B.C., believed that they had been given the right to rule by heaven. The king's duties included performing rituals to maintain harmony between heaven and the terrestrial world. During the Han dynasty (206 B.C.–A.D. 220), nobles were buried in elaborate tombs with objects for use in the afterlife, such as mirrors, which symbolized the universe. A silk tomb banner illustrates the Chinese belief in three realms: an underworld, a terrestrial world, and heaven.

RITUAL AX, ZHOU PERIOD

BRONZE RITUAL VESSELS, SHANG DYNASTY

Owl with "ears"

Post with flared top

Lid with raised decoration

Handle

Stylized monster mask

Splayed leg

JIA (VESSEL FOR WINE)

Knob

Beak-shaped handle

Owl's wing

Raised decoration in the shape of an owl

Little deer

ZUN (VESSEL FOR WINE)

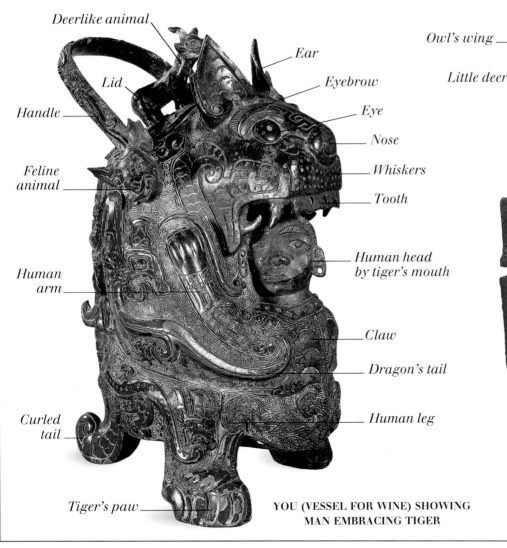

Deerlike animal

Ear

Lid

Eyebrow

Handle

Eye

Nose

Feline animal

Whiskers

Tooth

Human head by tiger's mouth

Human arm

Claw

Dragon's tail

Human leg

Curled tail

Tiger's paw

YOU (VESSEL FOR WINE) SHOWING MAN EMBRACING TIGER

Inscription

Handle

Snake decoration

Raised boss

Water-buffalo or ox head

FANG DING (VESSEL FOR FOOD)

DETAIL FROM LOWER SECTION OF SILK BANNER

Dragon's claw

Jing chime-stone

Bi-disk, a symbol of heaven

Entwined dragon

Attendant

Table with winged cups

Ding vessel

Tortoise, a symbol of longevity

Objects for the afterlife

Snake

Mythical creature

Owl

Fish

Giant holding up the terrestrial world

SILK BANNER SHOWING MYTHOLOGICAL JOURNEY TO HEAVEN, FROM TOMB AT MAWANGDUI, HAN DYNASTY

Goddess with human body and serpent's tail

Red Sun, a symbol of the yang essence

Raven, a symbol of the Sun

White rabbit, a symbol of the Moon

Toad, a symbol of the Moon

Moon, a symbol of the yin essence

Lady representing the mythological Chang'e fleeing to the Moon

Gateway to heaven

Scene of heaven

Small sun

Guardian of the heavenly gate

Dragon

Attendant kneeling

One of three attendants

Limit of the terrestrial world

Owner of tomb

Human-headed spirit

Giant holding up the terrestrial world

Attendants with objects for the afterlife

ORACLE BONE, SHANG DYNASTY

Inscription of a question and response, the diviner's name, and a cyclical date

Burn mark where a hot poker was applied to a carved hole

Crack

Carved hole

FRONT VIEW

BACK VIEW

BRONZE MIRROR, HAN DYNASTY

Round shape representing heaven

Boss representing the terrestrial world's central mountain

Auspicious inscription

Square representing the terrestrial world

Japan

IN THE FOURTH CENTURY, a number of small Japanese kingdoms were unified under a single ruler. Over the next three centuries, the Japanese imperial line was established, as was Shinto, the native religion. This period, known as the Kofun (Old Tomb) period, was characterized by the building of huge tombs. These tombs were surrounded by haniwa—clay models in the shape of human figures, horses, and other objects. Stoneware, called Sue ware, was placed inside the tombs. During the Kofun period, Japan received important cultural influences from China and Korea. Chinese-style writing was adopted by the early sixth century and Buddhism had reached Japan from Korea by the mid sixth century. Buddhism was popularized by Crown Prince Shotoku (574–622). He encouraged the building of temples and monasteries, such as Hōryū-ji, which he founded in 607 (although this temple was later rebuilt). In time, Buddhist temples came to be regarded as symbols of prestige. Buddhism also introduced new styles of art and architecture. Temples held treasures such as statues of the Buddha and bodhisattvas (Buddhist deities), and sutras, which were scrolls of holy Buddhist texts.

BRONZE DOTAKU BELLS

EMPEROR NINTOKU'S TOMB, OSAKA

Second moat

Ancillary tomb

Main burial mound

Inner moat

Outer moat

Stone-lined passage to tomb

Row of haniwa for protection

HANIWA (EARTHENWARE TOMB MODELS)

Helmet of riveted iron plates

Neck protector

Armor of laced iron plates

Protective shoulder plate

Arm protector

Bow

Hip armor of laced iron plates

Single-edged sword

Leg armor of laced iron plates

Cylindrical base

HANIWA WARRIOR

Wooden saddle

Bridle

HANIWA HORSE

Jar

Ritual cup

Wrestlers

Cut-out slot

Pedestal

SUE WARE JAR AND PEDESTAL

Ornamental bargeboard

Hip-and-gable roof

Thatched roof

Window

Raised floor

HANIWA NOBLEMAN'S HOUSE

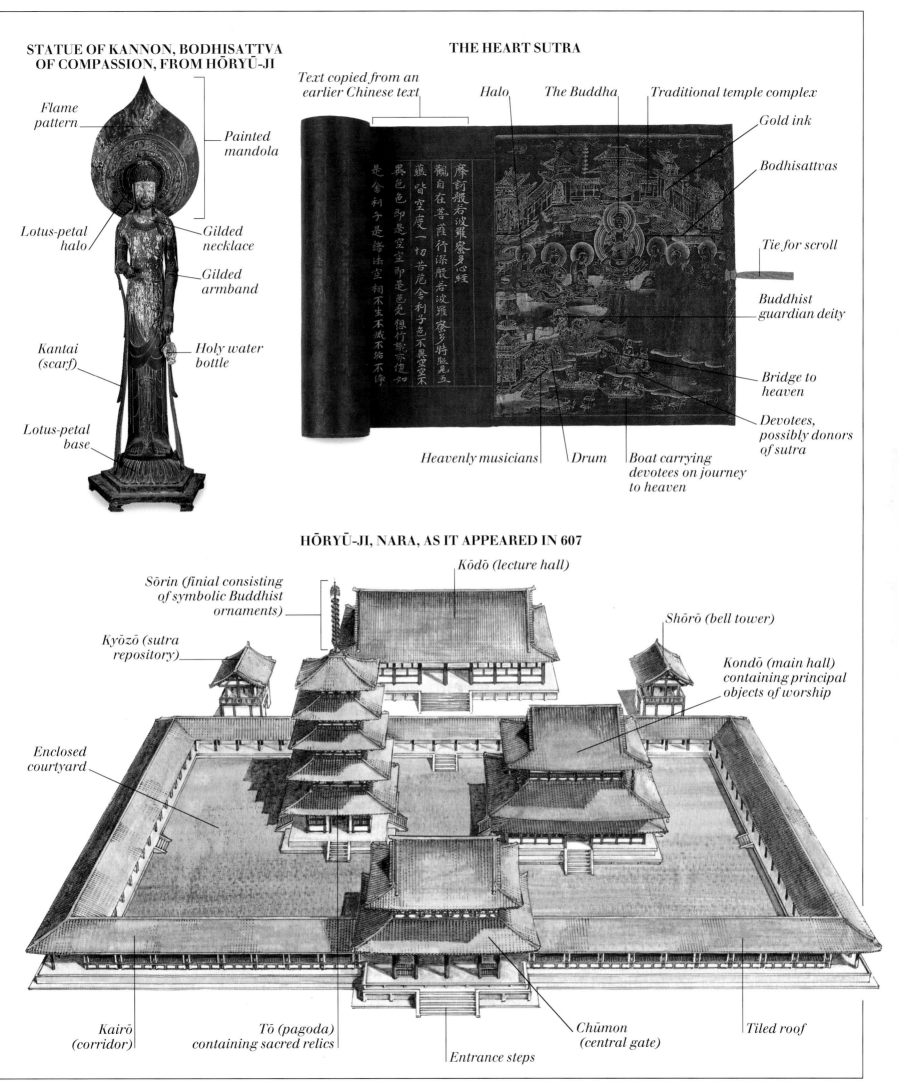

STATUE OF KANNON, BODHISATTVA OF COMPASSION, FROM HŌRYŪ-JI

Flame pattern

Painted mandola

Lotus-petal halo

Gilded necklace

Gilded armband

Kantai (scarf)

Holy water bottle

Lotus-petal base

THE HEART SUTRA

Text copied from an earlier Chinese text

Halo

The Buddha

Traditional temple complex

Gold ink

Bodhisattvas

Tie for scroll

Buddhist guardian deity

Bridge to heaven

Devotees, possibly donors of sutra

Heavenly musicians

Drum

Boat carrying devotees on journey to heaven

摩訶般若波羅蜜多心経
觀自在菩薩行深般若波羅蜜多時照見五
蘊皆空度一切苦厄舍利子色不異空空不
異色色即是空空即是色受想行識亦復如
是舎利子是諸法空相不生不滅不垢不淨

HŌRYŪ-JI, NARA, AS IT APPEARED IN 607

Kōdō (lecture hall)

Sōrin (finial consisting of symbolic Buddhist ornaments)

Kyōzō (sutra repository)

Shōrō (bell tower)

Kondō (main hall) containing principal objects of worship

Enclosed courtyard

Kairō (corridor)

Tō (pagoda) containing sacred relics

Chūmon (central gate)

Entrance steps

Tiled roof

55

Timelines 1

The timelines on these pages show most of the civilizations and cultures featured in this book within a chronological framework. Other cultures, not included in this book, are also shown to give an indication of what was happening simultaneously in different parts of the world. The charts are divided vertically into successive time periods, beginning with 3500 B.C. and ending at A.D. 1600. The civilizations are shown extending across pages in one of five geographical regions: the Americas, Australasia and Oceania, the Middle East and Africa, Europe, and India and the Far East. The approximate area of each region is shown on the maps on pages 56 and 58. The principal civilizations within a particular region—for example, Greece and Rome within Europe—are distinguished by a color code, which is also shown on the maps. The illustrations show some of the artistic, cultural, and architectural achievements of the different civilizations.

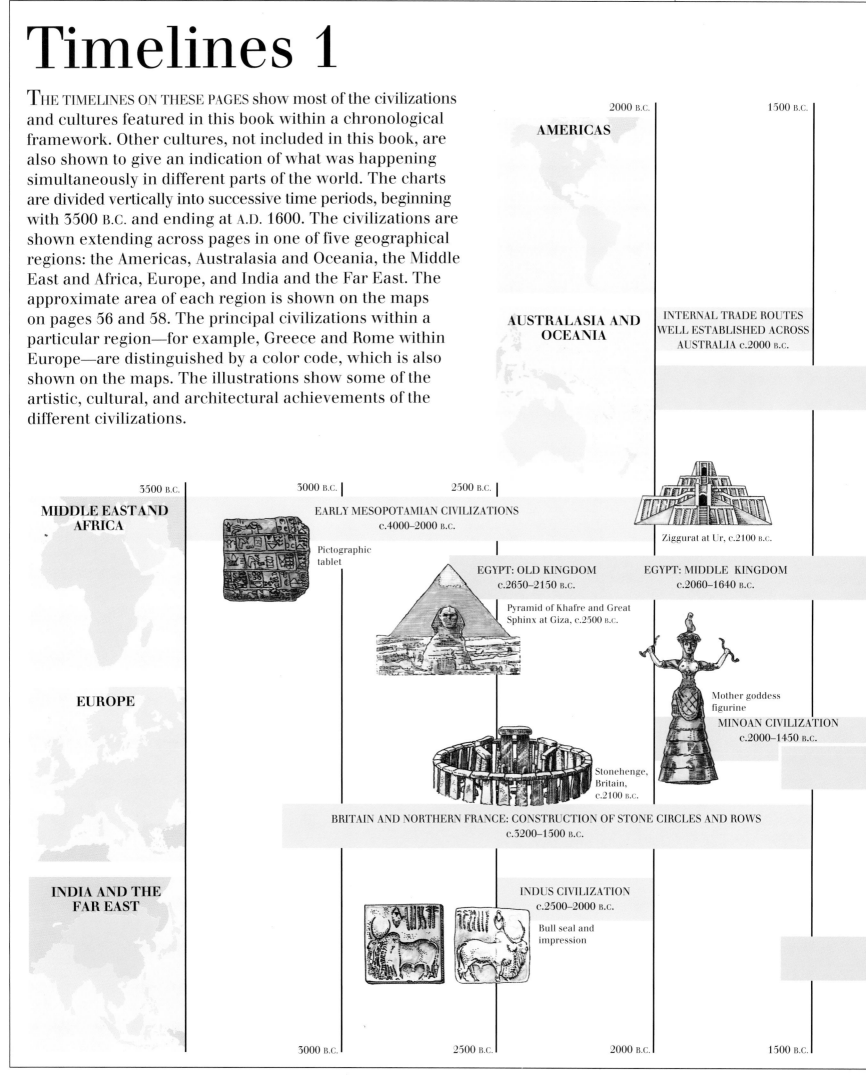

2000 B.C.   1500 B.C.

AMERICAS

AUSTRALASIA AND OCEANIA

INTERNAL TRADE ROUTES WELL ESTABLISHED ACROSS AUSTRALIA c.2000 B.C.

Ziggurat at Ur, c.2100 B.C.

3500 B.C.   3000 B.C.   2500 B.C.

MIDDLE EAST AND AFRICA

EARLY MESOPOTAMIAN CIVILIZATIONS
c.4000–2000 B.C.

Pictographic tablet

EGYPT: OLD KINGDOM
c.2650–2150 B.C.

EGYPT: MIDDLE KINGDOM
c.2060–1640 B.C.

Pyramid of Khafre and Great Sphinx at Giza, c.2500 B.C.

Mother goddess figurine

EUROPE

MINOAN CIVILIZATION
c.2000–1450 B.C.

Stonehenge, Britain, c.2100 B.C.

BRITAIN AND NORTHERN FRANCE: CONSTRUCTION OF STONE CIRCLES AND ROWS
c.3200–1500 B.C.

INDIA AND THE FAR EAST

INDUS CIVILIZATION
c.2500–2000 B.C.

Bull seal and impression

3000 B.C.   2500 B.C.   2000 B.C.   1500 B.C.

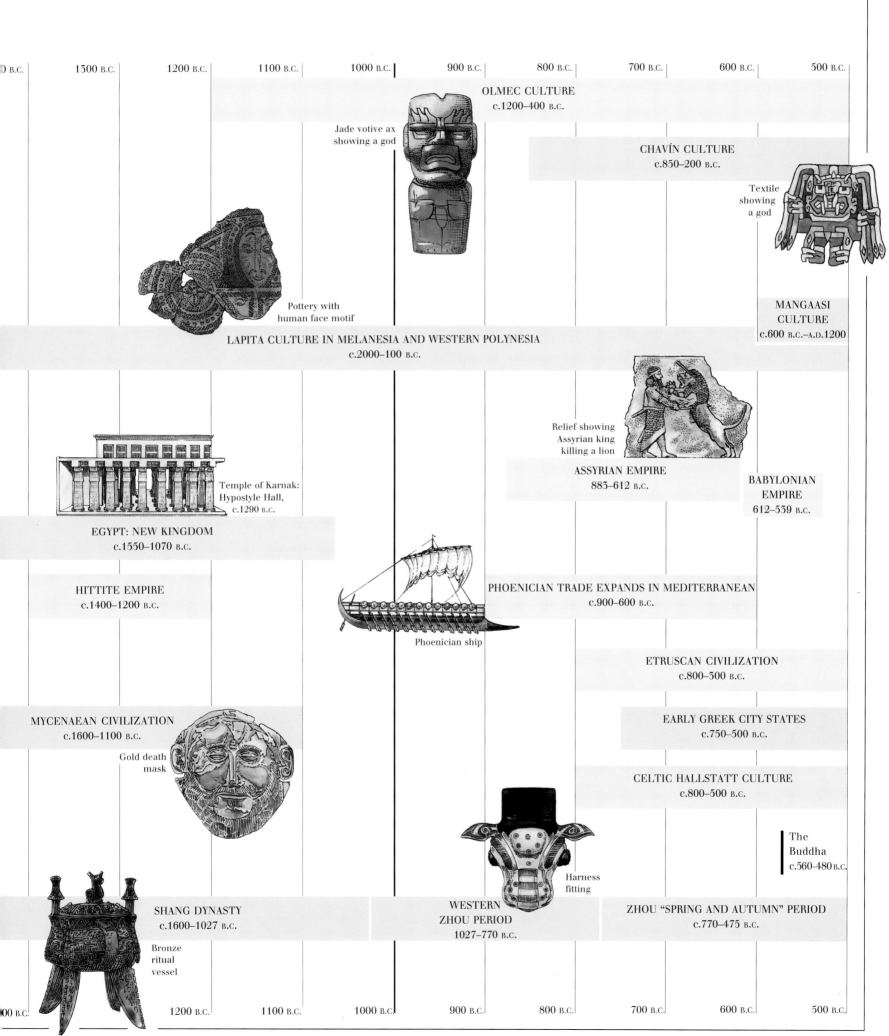

OLMEC CULTURE
c.1200–400 B.C.

Jade votive ax
showing a god

CHAVÍN CULTURE
c.850–200 B.C.

Textile
showing
a god

Pottery with
human face motif

**MANGAASI
CULTURE**
c.600 B.C.–A.D.1200

LAPITA CULTURE IN MELANESIA AND WESTERN POLYNESIA
c.2000–100 B.C.

Relief showing
Assyrian king
killing a lion

Temple of Karnak:
Hypostyle Hall,
c.1290 B.C.

ASSYRIAN EMPIRE
883–612 B.C.

**BABYLONIAN
EMPIRE**
612–539 B.C.

EGYPT: NEW KINGDOM
c.1550–1070 B.C.

HITTITE EMPIRE
c.1400–1200 B.C.

PHOENICIAN TRADE EXPANDS IN MEDITERRANEAN
c.900–600 B.C.

Phoenician ship

ETRUSCAN CIVILIZATION
c.800–500 B.C.

MYCENAEAN CIVILIZATION
c.1600–1100 B.C.

Gold death
mask

EARLY GREEK CITY STATES
c.750–500 B.C.

CELTIC HALLSTATT CULTURE
c.800–500 B.C.

The
Buddha
c.560–480 B.C.

Harness
fitting

SHANG DYNASTY
c.1600–1027 B.C.

**WESTERN
ZHOU PERIOD**
1027–770 B.C.

ZHOU "SPRING AND AUTUMN" PERIOD
c.770–475 B.C.

Bronze
ritual
vessel

Timelines 2

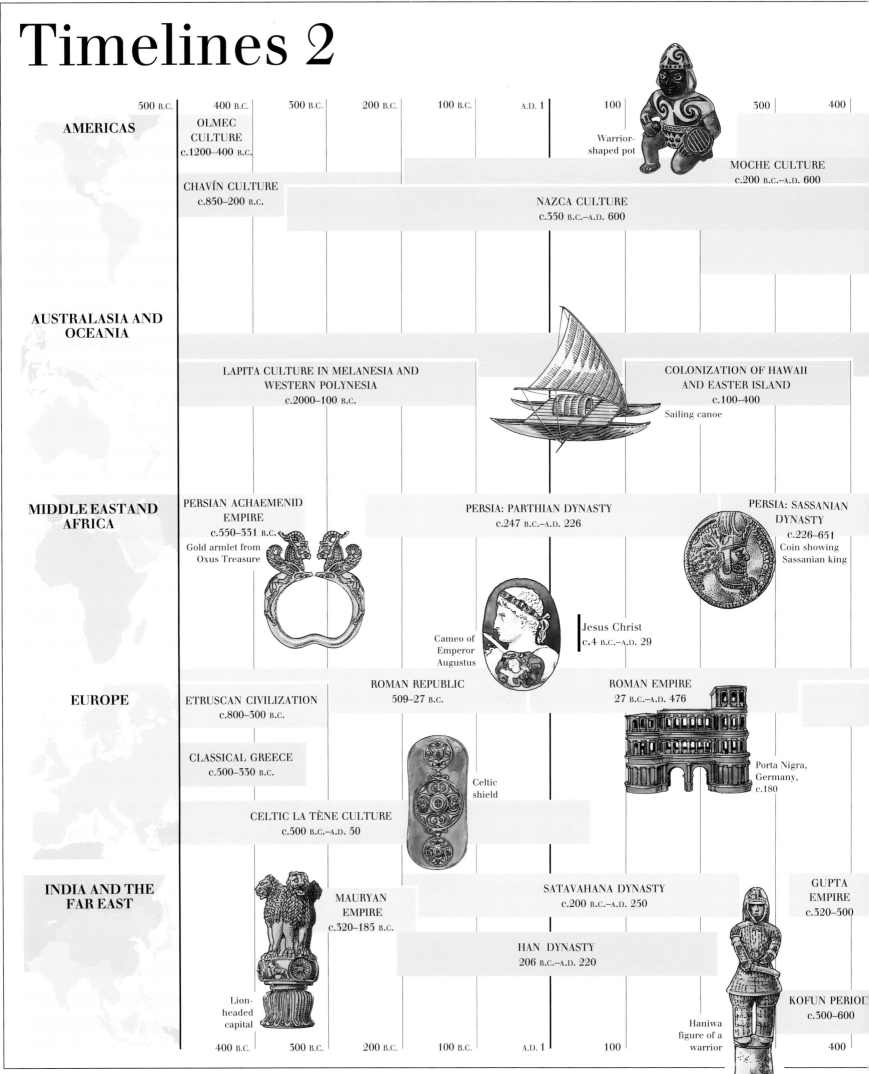

| | 500 B.C. | 400 B.C. | 300 B.C. | 200 B.C. | 100 B.C. | A.D. 1 | 100 | 300 | 400 |

AMERICAS

OLMEC CULTURE
c.1200–400 B.C.

CHAVÍN CULTURE
c.850–200 B.C.

NAZCA CULTURE
c.350 B.C.–A.D. 600

Warrior-shaped pot

MOCHE CULTURE
c.200 B.C.–A.D. 600

AUSTRALASIA AND OCEANIA

LAPITA CULTURE IN MELANESIA AND WESTERN POLYNESIA
c.2000–100 B.C.

COLONIZATION OF HAWAII AND EASTER ISLAND
c.100–400

Sailing canoe

MIDDLE EAST AND AFRICA

PERSIAN ACHAEMENID EMPIRE
c.550–331 B.C.

Gold armlet from Oxus Treasure

PERSIA: PARTHIAN DYNASTY
c.247 B.C.–A.D. 226

PERSIA: SASSANIAN DYNASTY
c.226–651

Coin showing Sassanian king

Cameo of Emperor Augustus

Jesus Christ
c.4 B.C.–A.D. 29

EUROPE

ETRUSCAN CIVILIZATION
c.800–300 B.C.

ROMAN REPUBLIC
509–27 B.C.

ROMAN EMPIRE
27 B.C.–A.D. 476

CLASSICAL GREECE
c.500–330 B.C.

Celtic shield

Porta Nigra, Germany, c.180

CELTIC LA TÈNE CULTURE
c.500 B.C.–A.D. 50

INDIA AND THE FAR EAST

MAURYAN EMPIRE
c.320–185 B.C.

SATAVAHANA DYNASTY
c.200 B.C.–A.D. 250

GUPTA EMPIRE
c.320–500

HAN DYNASTY
206 B.C.–A.D. 220

Lion-headed capital

Haniwa figure of a warrior

KOFUN PERIOD
c.300–600

| | 400 B.C. | 300 B.C. | 200 B.C. | 100 B.C. | A.D. 1 | 100 | 400 |

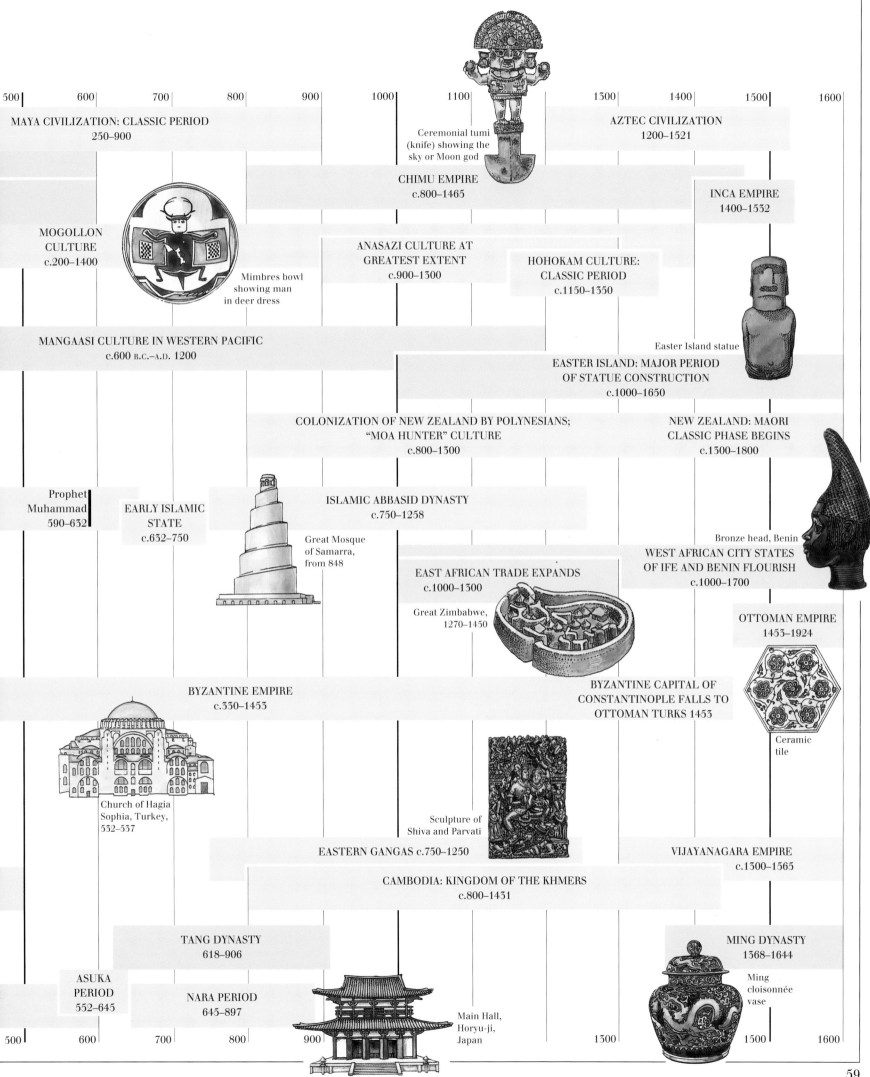

500 600 700 800 900 1000 1100 1300 1400 1500 1600

MAYA CIVILIZATION: CLASSIC PERIOD
250–900

AZTEC CIVILIZATION
1200–1521

Ceremonial tumi
(knife) showing the
sky or Moon god

CHIMU EMPIRE
c.800–1465

INCA EMPIRE
1400–1532

**MOGOLLON
CULTURE**
c.200–1400

**ANASAZI CULTURE AT
GREATEST EXTENT**
c.900–1300

**HOHOKAM CULTURE:
CLASSIC PERIOD**
c.1150–1350

Mimbres bowl
showing man
in deer dress

MANGAASI CULTURE IN WESTERN PACIFIC
c.600 B.C.–A.D. 1200

Easter Island statue

**EASTER ISLAND: MAJOR PERIOD
OF STATUE CONSTRUCTION**
c.1000–1650

**COLONIZATION OF NEW ZEALAND BY POLYNESIANS;
"MOA HUNTER" CULTURE**
c.800–1300

**NEW ZEALAND: MAORI
CLASSIC PHASE BEGINS**
c.1300–1800

Prophet
Muhammad
590–632

**EARLY ISLAMIC
STATE**
c.632–750

ISLAMIC ABBASID DYNASTY
c.750–1258

Bronze head, Benin

**WEST AFRICAN CITY STATES
OF IFE AND BENIN FLOURISH**
c.1000–1700

Great Mosque
of Samarra,
from 848

EAST AFRICAN TRADE EXPANDS
c.1000–1300

Great Zimbabwe,
1270–1450

OTTOMAN EMPIRE
1453–1924

BYZANTINE EMPIRE
c.330–1453

**BYZANTINE CAPITAL OF
CONSTANTINOPLE FALLS TO
OTTOMAN TURKS 1453**

Ceramic
tile

Church of Hagia
Sophia, Turkey,
532–537

Sculpture of
Shiva and Parvati

EASTERN GANGAS c.750–1250

VIJAYANAGARA EMPIRE
c.1300–1565

CAMBODIA: KINGDOM OF THE KHMERS
c.800–1431

TANG DYNASTY
618–906

MING DYNASTY
1368–1644

Ming
cloisonnée
vase

**ASUKA
PERIOD
552–645**

**NARA PERIOD
645–897**

Main Hall,
Horyu-ji,
Japan

500 600 700 800 900 1300 1500 1600

Index

Acknowledgments

Dorling Kindersley would like to thank:
The Trustees and the staff of the Departments of the British Museum, London, in particular James Putnam, Anne Farrer, Herma Chang, and Jim Hamill; The National Trust; Frances Wood of the British Library, London

Picture credits:
(t=top, b=bottom, c=center, l=left, r=right)
All photography from the British Museum, London except for:
Archiv fur Kunst front cover, 24cr (Herakleion Museum, Crete); 25t (Erich Lessing, National Archeological Museum, Athens); front cover, 18tr (Erich Lessing, Louvre Museum, Paris).
Ashmolean Museum, Oxford front cover; 6tl; 20tl; 25bl.
Collection Tony Berlant, Santa Monica, CA 5cr; 45cr.
Dr. J. Biel, Landesdemkmalant Baden-Württemberg, Stuttgart 22cl; 22b.
Bildarchiv Preussischer Kulturbesitz 19 (Klaus Goken, Berlin State Museum).
Bridgeman Art Library 21b (Louvre Museum, Paris).
British Library Board, London 53bl.
Cambridge University Museum of Archaeology and Anthropology 40tr; 42tl; 43tr.
Andy Crawford 34tl.
Darmstadt Museum 34-35b; 35t.
C.M. Dixon 24br (Herakleion Museum, Crete).
Werner Forman Archive 42tr (Museum für Völkerkunde, Berlin); 44tl (Arizona State Museum); 45tr (Maxwell Museum of Anthropology, Albuquerque).
James Harpur 26cl.
Michael Holford 42bl; 42br; 52bl (Cernuschi Museum, Paris).
Museums of Scotland 32tl; 37tcl; 54cc.
INAH, Mexican Museum Authority (Michel Zabé) 38bl; 38bc; 38br; 40tl; 41tr; 41br; 42br.
Image Bank (Charles C. Place) 45tl.
Justin Kerr, New York front cover; 2–3bc; 38tr; 39.
The National Trust 5br; 48bl.
Ruth Midgley 24tl.
Peabody Museum, Harvard University (Hillel Burger) 44tcr; 44tr; 45br.
Royal Photographic Society (Francis Frith) 11cl.
Sir John Soanes Museum, London 26b.
Scala, Florence 24bl (Herakleion Museum, Crete); 28tl (National Museum of Athens); 32br (Vatican); 33; 36br (Uffizi).
The Science Museum, London 34bl.

Collection of the Tokyo National Museum 54bl; 54bc; 54r.
University of Tennessee 10-11b.

Additional photography:
Alan Hills, Ivor Kerslake, David Gower, Nick Nicholls, Peter Hayman, Kevin Lovelock, Christi Graham (The British Museum); Michel Zabé; Geoff Brightling; Karl Shone

Additional editorial assistance:
David Harding

Additional artwork:
Russell Barnett 34

Index:
Kay Wright

Picture Research:
Valya Alexander; Caroline Brooke